Overthinking

The Ultimate Guide to Stop Negative Thoughts, Stress and Anxiety. Declutter Your Mind, Start Thinking Positively to Finally Improve Your Life.

Jennet Brown

Table of Contents

Introduction

Traumatic though, as we all witness, can be challenging to categorize as the unpleasant and foreign adversary it is. We will criticize ourselves for hours over little things from our day without understanding how unrealistic and cruel we are being. We will question our vital inner voice and potentially alter our way of thinking by noticing these emotions and knowing when they are stimulated. Standing up against the inner critic needs three key steps: It's useful to verbalize what the damaging coach in your mind is teaching you anytime you find yourself overthinking. Do you have negative feelings about yourself, criticizing your job performance? "In today's conference, you sounded so dumb. All believe you have no idea what you're doing right now. You're a knucklehead! "If you just put your head down, no one will hear you." The coach may even be deceptive and seem to be self-soothing. "You should unwind. You are not needed to complete the project tonight. You've earned a rest. Just sit down and have a drink." That same soothing-sounding accent, on the other hand, will turn on a dime and scold you for not meeting your objectives. "You're such a slug. Look at you; you've spent the whole night lounging around. You never want to get much done." Both self-defeating and self-calming voices contribute to the same unfavorable result. That is why it is important to pay attention to these ideas. Take note of when they appear and what they're trying to tell you. You may see a trend as you become conscious of the particular thoughts you have about yourself or others. Do you find yourself being harsher on your partner when he or she brings up a certain topic? When you're talking to your child, dad, boss, sibling, or girlfriend, do you turn on yourself? If you understand the many kinds of vital inner voices you're hearing, you should consider the true root of these reflections. They can surprise you to find that they have very little to do with you and your true feelings in your current life or circumstance. Did anybody, for example, regard you as a child as if you were stupid or incapable? Were you advised to be self-sufficient or not to put your faith in others? All of your parents' or other powerful early caregivers' attitudes toward themselves and you will seep into your consciousness and manifest as your vital inner voice. Understanding that these attitudes come from will assist you in distinguishing them from your true viewpoint while still allowing you to have greater compassion for yourself.

Chapter 1 What Is Overthinking, Anyway?

Overthinking is just as it sounds like: thinking so hard. Overthinking is where you keep repeating the same idea, analyzing all the simplest scenarios or events until you lose all sense of proportion since the overthinking brain is unable to convert these emotions into acts or beneficial consequences, depression and anxiety result.

Find out all about anxiety hypnotherapy here. I'm also providing a free initial consultation, which you can schedule here.

Is it possible that I'm overthinking things?

Isn't it true that we all overthink things to some extent? Worrying over stuff is tied to thinking about our loved ones and doing a decent job as parents, sons or daughters, workers or business owners.

Those who have a serious problem with overthinking are known as "ruminators," who obsess over past incidents. Worrying about the future is common: will I be able to reach this deadline? Is it possible for me to locate a suitable residential apartment for my mother? Worries will also help us move on when we figure out how to deal with them; nevertheless, overthinking is more defensive than aggressive, focusing on previous experiences and projecting disproportionately pessimistic potential outcomes.

Consider the following scenario. You call your new manager by the wrong name by mistake. When realize is this later, what do you think and feel?

The typical worrier will be slightly humiliated, intend to apologize the next day with a self-deprecating remark, then forget about it and cook dinner. The overthinker will repeat the mistake several times, rewriting new results each time. By four a.m., he or she will imagine situations in which he or she will be passed over for potential promotions or even selected for redundancy. The incident has sparked a flurry of major questions in the overthinking imagination, exaggerating the severity of the situation.

This may seem to be a minor example, but it illustrates how over-thinking can take over multiple aspects of your life. The classic manifestations of what an overthinking mind can do are dwelling on a previous occurrence and drawing tragic conclusions from it.

Overthinking is caused by the brain's primitive emotional core. Overthinking, like many much anxieties depression symptoms, stems from one of our primal survival instincts.

The primitive mind would still see life in the most negative light possible. This is because the brain is trying to keep us alive by being hyper-vigilant – there's no point in being positive about those saber-too.

The rational brain will remind us that we will not risk our jobs because we mispronounce our boss's name on the other hand people who ruminate, are reacting in a primal fight-or-flight mode, where dwelling on the worst-case situations is more likely to keep us alive. Anxiety and overthinking work together to amplify feelings of tension and helplessness.

Overthinking adds to the tension level.

It's easy to instill fear by making pessimistic predictions about the future. Reminiscing about the past, on the other hand, will make one feel incredibly nervous. Negative emotions overflow our "stress bucket" to the point that we believe one more trickle, one more thought, will cause us to burst.

How can we get rid of the tension of our lives? At night, we undergo the miraculous healing phase of REM sleep, in which our minds review the activities of the day and transfer them from the physical, primitive brain to the intellectual side. The brain records events, including emotion and suppressed emotion, and stores them as memories and narratives for later. As part of this phase, the brain can also 'live out' unspent emotion by dreaming in order to use up unspent adrenalin. The individual who misidentified their manager will not forget the incident overnight, but they will not be worrying about it in the morning.

The one who thinks so much would not be so lucky. If he or she is not sleeping well due to overthinking, tossing and turning while ruminating about the events, they will miss out on this essential REM sleep, waking up through the night or not being able to fall asleep until the early hours of the morning, at which point it will be time to get up to start the day with low energy and a bad mood.

How hypnotherapy with a solution-focused approach will help you from overthinking

All worries too much at times. People who find it impossible to interrupt their emotions face difficulties. While the odd over-thinker may be able to rationalize the original concern, the true ruminator is constantly bombarded by pessimistic thoughts. It's all too easy to fall into a negative cycle, when heightened anxiety leads to more overthinking, and so on.

As a result, we must interrupt the loop. With its emphasis on the current and future, solution-based hypnotherapy is a logical approach to combat overthinking. We enter a state where all sides of the brain come together as we create a contrived trance state, and this is where we will begin to substitute all of these negative emotions with hopeful thoughts about the future.

We discuss strategies and paths forward, assisting you in setting attainable targets, recognizing and building on your talents and resources, and identifying moments that you are doing well.

Hypnosis, in and of itself, decreases fear by encouraging individuals to concentrate on the good facets of their lives, resulting in a turn toward a more hopeful – and rational – outlook.

The new boss you named by the wrong name by accident? It's provided an excellent opportunity for a casual conversation, which is always a good thing, right?

Let's start debating overthinking – as a group.
You're not the only one who feels this way. Overthinking is a problem that many people have, and I will help you solve it.

Solution-based hypnotherapy will quickly break the loop of overthinking and fear. This is a normal, relaxing, and secure way to reclaim control of your emotions.

When Do You knows you're Overthinking?
It can be overwhelming to consider all the things you should have done better, to second-guess any decision you make, and to imagine all the worst-case situations in life. Overthinking, on the other hand, is a difficult practice to overcome.

You might also persuade yourself that spending a lot of time worrying about something is the trick to coming up with the right idea, but this is rarely the case.

In reality, the more time and energy you spend thinking about something, the less time and energy you have to act on it.

Of course, everybody worries so much at times. Perhaps you constantly imagine all the stuff that could go wrong when you make a presentation next week.

Maybe you spent so much time figuring out what to wear to the work interview that you didn't have time to prepare your responses.

You must first know that you are overthinking before you can stop it. Here's how to tell whether you're overthinking anything.

You Aren't Solution-Oriented

Problem-solving is not the same as overthinking. Problem-solving entails searching for a solution, while overthinking entails focusing on the problem.

Assume a hurricane is approaching. The distinction between overthinking and problem-solving is as follows:

• Overthinking: "I'm hoping the hurricane can pass us by." It's going to be a disaster. I'm hoping the house isn't harmed. Why does this stuff have to happen to me all of the time? This is too much for me."

• Fixing problems: "I'll go outside and pick up something that could fly up." To deter flooding, I'll place sandbags against the garage door. I'll go to the supermarket and buy plywood to cover up the windows if we have a lot of rain."

Solving problems can lead to positive outcomes. Overthinking, on the other hand, fuels unpleasant thoughts while obstructing the search for answers.

You Have a Lot of Repetitive Thoughts

Ruminating—or rehashing the same issues over and over—isn't productive. When you're overthinking, though, you may find yourself replaying a conversation or remembering something bad happening constantly in your mind.

You're more likely to ruminate on your feelings as your mental health deteriorates. It's a vicious trap that's difficult to crack.

Your anxiety keeps you awake at night

When you're overthinking, your brain will sound as though it won't turn off. When you go to relax, you can feel as if your brain is working overtime, replaying scenes in your mind and making you imagine negative things.

Rumination keeps you awake at night, according to research. Overthinking makes it difficult to relax.

Overthinking will also affect the consistency of your sleep. As a result, falling into a deep slumber is more difficult when the mind is preoccupied with overthinking everything. 2

Falling asleep can be difficult, and can lead to more worrying feelings. When you don't fall asleep right away, for example, you can worry that you'll be overtired the next day. This can make you feel uncomfortable, making falling asleep even more difficult.

You Find It Difficult to Make Decisions
You might attempt to persuade yourself that thought more deeply and over longer periods of time is beneficial. After all, you're examining a dilemma from any perspective possible.

Overanalyzing and obsessing, on the other hand, becomes a roadblock. According to research, overthinking makes it difficult to make decisions.

You may be overthinking stuff if you're indecisive on everything from what to eat for dinner to which hotel to book.

It's very likely that you're squandering time seeking second opinions and exploring your alternatives because, in the end, those minor decisions do not matter all that much.

Why Do People Get Obsessed With Things?
Overthinking will lead to you berating yourself for choices you've already taken.

You could spend a lot of time fantasizing about how much easier your life would be if you had just taken some other job or not started a company. Or maybe you blame yourself for not seeing red flags earlier, believing that they should have been apparent!

Rehashing and second-guessing is a kind of mental punishment, whereas a little positive self-reflection will help you learn from your mistakes.

Overthinking will depress the attitude and make making decisions even more challenging in the future.

What to Do If You're Always Overthinking

According to research, worrying less about a problem might be the trick to coming up with better solutions. According to research, giving yourself an "incubation time" will help you make the right choices.

Distracting Yourself Can Be Beneficial

Rather than sitting and thinking about a topic for an indefinite period of time, you should divert your attention for a while.

When you're busy with another job, such as gardening, your brain might find better ways to figure out a solution in the background. You might even "sleep on it," in which case the brain would fix the dilemma for you as you sleep.

You will take a rest for a quick diversion. It can even help you concentrate on something more positive. When you stop worrying about the situation, your brain might even come up with a solution for you.

If you're having trouble breaking loose from overthinking, seek therapeutic assistance. Overthinking may be a sign of a mental illness such as depression or anxiety. On the other hand, it may raise the risk of having mental health issues.

A mental health specialist will show you techniques to help you from obsessing, ruminating, and focusing on unhelpful thoughts. They can also assist you in identifying effective coping mechanisms, such as mindfulness or physical activity.

Consult the doctor if you believe your brain is working overtime. Your psychiatrist will be able to recommend a professional who will assist you with overcoming your overthinking.

Overthinking and Its Consequences For Mental And Physical Health

Overthinking isn't a medicinal concept in and of itself, but evidence suggests that the practice may have severe consequences for our health. Overthinking often means reflecting on the negative — rehashing the past, dwelling on negative events, or fretting about the future.

When we ruminate on those ideas, says Ashley Carroll, a psychologist at Parkland Memorial Hospital, it can snowball into larger, more intense negative thinking. Overthinking, according to Carroll, becomes a concern as it begins to interfere with daily life.

"Whether it becomes harmful to our lives or seriously impairs our daily functioning," Carroll said. "For example, if you have trouble sleeping at night and you can't keep these feelings off, that's affecting your daily functioning." "If it's upsetting your appetite, if you're being isolated from other people because you're too stuck in your thoughts..."

Carroll believes that ruminating on the worst-case situations and consequences is a misguided way of self-defense.

"It can be a defensive mechanism for certain individuals," she said. "'So I'm going to presume that someone is untrustworthy instantly, so I won't get attached to anybody and can defend myself."

Carroll claims that overthinking will have a negative impact on one's physical health. She said that some of her patients who struggle with suicidal feelings and anxiety often have insomnia, body aches, and digestive issues. Overthinking has also been linked to mental health conditions such as depression, anxiety, PTSD, and borderline personality disorder.

Carroll recommends taking care of what causes your overthinking as a first step toward breaking the pattern. It may be the result of a childhood experience or a new cause of tension in your life. Carroll suggests that after you've identified the causes, you will work on overcoming them.

"Whenever patients get into the ruminating cycle," she says, "I still recommend deep breathing exercises." "It assists them in refocusing their attention on their breathing and relaxing their central nervous system. Then [activities] like journaling help them articulate and organize the emotions that are running through their minds. So any mindfulness activity in which you're really concentrating on the current moment will prevent you from thinking about the past or the future."

Are you a thinker who thinks so much?

Have your feelings ever made you feel overwhelmed? Many of my clients have shown dissatisfaction, if not outright anguish, with their self-imposed psychiatric questioning. It manifests as an uncontrollable need to examine virtually everything they think, especially the unexpected, unexpected thoughts that arise out of nowhere.

Consider the case of Jessica, a young adult. She tried anxiety therapy, but it was apparent after a brief time that she was trapped in a self-defeating emotional bind. Any negative, unwelcome thinking prompted a torturous self-examination method.

"What prompted me to have this feeling," "what does it mean," "what if I get lost and get more and more nervous," or "I need to find a way to get better control of my mind," she'd ask herself over and over. She spent hours debating ideas that came to her out of nowhere. She'd still overthink what people said to her, constantly wondering whether they said something bad. Jessica said that she was "stuck in her brain."

Are you able to relate? Do you ever feel like you're stuck in a loop of overanalyzing your thoughts? Worry, rumination, and obsessive thoughts are also symptoms of overthinking. However, it is not confined to these circumstances. It can be a concern in and of itself, but few people realize how detrimental it can be to our emotional stability, satisfaction, and well-being. Many people believe that overthinking is a psychological trait; they are unaware that there are ways to combat this anxiety-inducing habit.

Overthinking Symptoms

If you're not sure if overthinking is a challenge for you, think about the following questions, which are based on a questionnaire I created for The Anxious Thoughts Workbook2:

• Do you have a good sense of what you're thinking at any given time?

• Do you ever wonder why you're thinking the way you are?

• Do you ever ponder the underlying meaning of your emotions or their emotional significance?

• Do you ever worry about what you're saying when you're upset?

• Do you have a keen desire to learn more about or comprehend how the mind works?

• Do you believe it is important to have complete control of your thoughts?

• Do you have a poor threshold for unwelcome feelings that come to you out of nowhere?

• Can you find it difficult to keep your emotions in check?

If you responded yes to several of these questions, you might have an overthinking problem.

There are two risks associated with this. You will get caught in indecision, avoidance, and procrastination if you overthink crucial problems in your life. Spending time in reflective contemplation on relationships, fitness, career, self-identity problems, and other topics is necessary, but spending so much time in one's mind can be expensive. However, we all have cynical, distracting feelings that can be ignored. Spending so much time thinking about these things will cause a lot of pain.

Overthinking and How to Avoid It

There are some precautions you may take if you believe you're succumbing to overthinking:

• Be aware of your personal causes. Also the most zealous overthinkers don't always do it. Overthinking is much more likely to be triggered by such feelings or problems. If you're a worrier, for example, worrying about the future will cause you to overthink things. For anyone else, it may be pondering their own competence or whether or not they are liked by others. Whatever the case might be, it's important to understand the "hot spots" that cause you to overthink.

• Recognize that you're overthinking anything. You must be aware of when you are overthinking in order to minimize it. What are the symptoms that you're worried about too much? Is that when you're trying to figure out what an intrusive thought means when there's no secret meaning? Is that when you're attempting to regulate or inhibit a thought too hard? Is that when the idea makes you feel scared or anxious? There could be other signs that you've fallen victim to overthinking.

• Accept its futility wholeheartedly. You'll never be able to stop overthinking as much as you find it's useful. Examine how you dealt with overthinking in the past and write down what worked for you. Is there some concrete answer or revelation as a result of your overthinking? Was there a greater number of positive or bad consequences?

• Take a break. Over-engagement with intrusive feelings is referred to as "too much in one's mind." Disengaging from the idea is the polar opposite solution. So, the easiest way to stop overthinking is to practice conscientious acceptance, which involves observing but not judging unwelcome feelings. A second strategy is a concentrated diversion, in which we divert our attention to a certain idea or task rather than attempting to overcome or comprehend the unwelcome thought we're overthinking.

Overthinking can be detrimental to our emotional well-being, especially when it is directed at unexpected, random, unpleasant emotions, photographs, or memories. Fortunately, through increasing our self-awareness and practicing mental disengagement, we will learn to control this unhelpful form of thought.

You Overthink All for Psychological Reasons

Our capacity to think objectively is a double-edged sword that we'd all does better to be more cautious of, whether it's anxiety about the future, ruminating on the past, or hypercriticism towards others.

However, before you try to resist overthinking, it's a good idea to figure out why you overthink in the first place.

Over the course of my career as a counselor, I've observed the following seven factors repeatedly in people who struggle with overthinking.

1. Early childhood education

The majority of people who have a serious habit of overthinking picked up the habit as a teenager. And they normally created it because it was the only way they could cope with frightening and stressful situations at the time.

As a child of an intoxicated father, for example, the practice of obsessively thinking about what would happen if dad came home drunk may have played a very useful role in keeping you safe or out of harm's way.

But there's a catch...

The original source of overthinking is always not the same as the ongoing cause.

While it's important to consider the root of your overthinking habit in the past, if you want to avoid overthinking, you must also understand what has you overthinking now...

2. The deception of command

Humans, rather than any other traumatic feeling, seem to have a particularly rough time dealing with helplessness. We despise being helpless!

This is particularly true when it comes to our loved ones—spouses, children, parents, employers, and so on. When someone we love or care for is in pain, we naturally want to assist them.

Unfortunately, our willingness to assist others is always much less than we would like to think. Many individuals, though, remain in ignorance of their helplessness rather than confronting it.

They think a lot, stress a lot, and ruminate a lot, even if they can't do much to help. And, although it isn't always beneficial, dreaming is almost always beneficial.

We overthink things to give us a sense of dominance and hold our helpless feelings at bay.

Sadly, the long-term risks are scarcely justified. Chronic anxiety stemming from constant worry; low self-esteem stemming from constant ruminating; depression and overwhelm stemming from never feeling able to turn off our brains.

Many of these can be traced back to our inability to tolerate helplessness. That is to say...

You must get more familiar with your loss of power if you wish to avoid overthinking.

3. The deception of assurance

The illusion of certainty, which is related to the illusion of dominance, is founded on the idea that another thing we humans can't bear is doubt.

We like to be secure about how things are going to turn out, particularly when there's a lot at stake. In reality, we sometimes turn to deception in order to avoid feeling confused, believing that things are more predictable than they are.

Overthinking is one form of denial of ambiguity...

Keeping ourselves in problem-solving mode gives one the impression that there is an answer if we just thought about it long and hard enough.

The essence of truth is all too much deeply ambiguous. The key is to recognize that confronting ambiguity head-on is the most effective way to deal with it in the long term.

You will only mitigate the negative impact of doubt on your life if you have the ability to deal with it.

4. Obsessiveness

Here's something most people don't get about perfectionism...

Being ideal isn't the aim of perfectionism. It's just about having the right feeling.

Perfectionists have a rough time going away from something they don't want and they don't think they're perfect:

• The article you're going to write on your blog.

• The paper that you're going to handoff.

• The piano piece you wish you could perform live in front of an audience.

Nobody thinks they ought to be flawless, which is clearly unlikely. However, they have a very poor threshold for feeling less than ideal for some material. And here's what happened...

Overthinking is a way for perfectionists to avoid having to feel less than ideal about their work.

If you persuade yourself that there's more to do, it's because there's more to care about. That means you'll spend less time feeling insecure and flawed.

If you suffer wfromperfectionism, it's likely that your overthinking is due to a lack of emotional tolerance.

Practice tolerating feelings of inadequacy so you can move on with your life regardless of how you're doing.

5. Added benefit
Some people fall into the trap of overthinking and it has unintended consequences.

- Some people continue to overthink because it elicits compassion and pity from other people in their life, which makes them feel good.

Overthinking can also be used as a justification for delaying or refusing decisions: if you convince yourself you can't make a decision because you haven't given it enough time, you can't be blamed for making a poor choice.

It's likely that you're overthinking and you're making something out of it.

So, one way to break the loop of overthinking is to find out what the non-obvious advantages of overthinking are, and then come up with less stressful ways to get the same result.

Perhaps you should focus on being more emotionally open and assertive in your relationship if you want to overthink because it gives you affection and sympathy from your partner.

Habits are formed for a cause. Understanding what the cause is is the first step in changing them.

6. Oversimplification
Overgeneralization occurs when you believe that when something works in one aspect of your life (for example, education or job), it will work in other areas as well (conflict with your partner or grief, for example).

The ability to think is a tool. However, sometimes people are so good at reasoning and are praised for it in many parts of life that they find it difficult to lay that tool down in other areas where it is not useful.

It's like the old adage goes, "All seems like a nail to a hammer."

To an experienced thinker, everything seems to be a dilemma that must be overcome with a lot of thought.

If you find yourself overthinking, make a list of different aspects of your life and objectively consider whether more critical thinking is the best solution.

7. Confrontation aversion

Conflict isn't something any of us like. As a result, we naturally want to stop it wherever possible.

Unfortunately, this means we don't get a lot of experience dealing with confrontation. As a result, we are less secure in our abilities to deal with confrontation effectively in the future.

As a result, we stop confrontation evermore....

Can you see where this loop is headed?

The trouble with constantly avoiding confrontation, like any phobia, is that you think conflict is always risky.

The fact that certain spiders are toxic does not mean that all spiders are dangerous. However, the longer you handle spiders in this manner, the more they will feel the same way.

So it is with conflict: the longer we suppress it irrationally, the more fearful we get of it.

And if you believe that any confrontation is risky, you'll waste a lot of time and mental resources each day trying to find out ways to prevent even minor conflicts. Then, once you've managed to stop it, you'll have to do a lot of emotional gymnastics to justify it.

Excessive fear of violence causes a lot of wasted thought.

There are some conflicts that you would stop at all costs. However, once you give yourself the time to train, the majority of it can be done well and with minimal discomfort.

Be prepared for a lot of internal strife if you insist on preventing external conflict.

What You Need to Know

It's good to consider that you fell into this pit in the first place if you want to avoid overthinking too much.

The following are the most important reasons I encounter:

• Childhood schooling • Illusions of power and assurance • Perfectionism • Secondary advantage • Overgeneralization • Dispute aversion

What Are the Causes of Overthinking?

What induces overthinking, and how can it be avoided?

Overthinking can be caused by a variety of factors. For example, we always worry about what other people will say if anything bad happens.

• Due to a lack of self-assurance.

• We believe that all problems are centered on us, and instead of fixing them, we keep overthinking them.

• Making up ridiculous scenarios that would never happen.

• We also feel mentally and mentally unwell as a result of anxiety.

• Always worrying about who we are and how we compare to others, which is a typical symptom of social and performance anxiety.

Anxiety problems include worrying — overthinking — a tumbling series of fears, abstract feelings, and clear thoughts, all of which can be handled with instincts.

Overthinking can be harmful.

The most fundamental and damaging consequence of overthinking is that we want to believe what we are overthinking.

How do I avoid overthinking?

You start protecting yourself from the beginning before overthinking begins to affect you better.

So how do you do it? Many people believe it's a mental issue that can't be solved.

How Can You Get Rid of Overthinking?

• bring something with you or around you to take your mind off things. Rather than arguing with or obsessing about your emotions, subtly change your focus to something else.

• Meditating: Guru of all medicine, if you like your mind is overbearing and obnoxious. Sitting in solitude and admiring tranquility a surefire way to achieve happiness.

• Physical activity: sweating while playing a sport or dancing will help you relax. And you'll feel revitalized and relieved.

• Read a book that promotes self-help and self-development. I would recommend Robin Sharma's book "Who Will Weep When You Die," which will actually change your perspective on life by including a list of

Overthinking acts as a deterrent because it comforts you in your unreal circumstances and increases negativity in your head, preventing you from following your good route.

Overthinking conjures up memories as well as contemplating lives. In any case, the urge to overthink anything prevents you from doing anything useful and serves as a roadblock.

Stop overthinking it and you'll fix 99 percent of the problems. So relax and take a deep breath! Life is about experiencing experiences rather than overthinking them.

Chapter 2 The connection between overthinking, anxiety, and negative thinking

Stress Factors

Your manager has been hounding you for turning in a paper plate, and you owe the IRS thousands of dollars you don't have. You're under a lot of pressure.

Stress Triggers Different people have different stress triggers. According to polls, work tension is at the top of the list. Forty percent of American employees confess to being stressed at work, and one-quarter believe work is the most stressful aspect of their lives.

Continue reading

Workplace stress can be caused by a variety of factors, including: • being dissatisfied with your career • having a heavy workload or too much obligation • working long hours • bad management, inconsistent work requirements, or having little say in the decision-making process

• Working in hazardous environments • Not knowing whether you'll be promoted or whether you'll be fired • Giving speeches in front of coworkers • Facing prejudice or abuse at work, particularly if the employer isn't supportive

Life's pressures will have a major effect as well. • The loss of a loved one • Divorce is an example of life pressures.

• A traumatic accident, such as a natural disaster, kidnapping, robbery, or abuse against you or a loved one • Getting married • Moving to a new home • Chronic illness or disability • Emotional issues (depression, anxiety, rage, sadness, remorse, low self-esteem) • Taking care of an elderly or disabled family member

Perhaps the source of stress is internal rather than external. Worrying over problems will cause you to become stressed. Any of these things will make you feel stressed:

• Doubt and fear When you hear about the possibility of terrorist threats, global warming, and dangerous substances on the news on a daily basis, it can make you feel depressed, particularly if you feel powerless to stop them. Even though disasters are usually occasional occurrences, their extensive coverage in the media can give the impression that they are more common than they are. Fears can also be more personal, such as worrying that you won't be able to complete a job at work or that you won't be able to cover your bills this month.

• Perceptions and attitudes. The way you see the environment or a certain event will influence whether or not it creates stress. If your television set is robbed, for example, and you adopt a negative mentality, "You'll be even less worried if you say, "It's OK, my insurance firm will pay for a new one!" than if you think, "My TV is off, and I'll never get it back!" What if the robbers return to my home to steal from me once more?" People who believe they are doing a good job at work will often be less stressed by a large upcoming project than someone who thinks they are inept.

• Standards that are unrealistic. No one is without flaws. If you expect to do it well all of the time, you'll get stressed out when things don't go as planned.

• Be open to change. Every big life transition, including a joyful occasion like a wedding or a work raise, can be traumatic. More stressful circumstances, such as a divorce, a major financial loss, or a family death, maybe major causes of stress.

Your stress level can vary depending on your attitude and how you respond to different circumstances. Some people are content to let life pass them by. Workplace and life stresses are mild stumbling blocks for them. Others are physically sick with anxiety.

Stress and the Consequences for Your Health

When you're in a tense environment, your body goes into overdrive. Your nervous system goes into overdrive, pumping out chemicals that brace you to fight or flee. It's known as the "fight or flight" reflex, and it's why, in a stressful situation, your pulse quickens, your breathing quickens, your muscles tense up, and you begin to sweat. This type of stress is only transient and short-lived (acute stress), and the body normally recovers rapidly.

Chronic stress, on the other hand, may contribute to or exacerbate more severe health issues if the stress response remains active for an extended period of time. The excessive influx of stress hormones will break down the body, allowing it to age faster and make you more susceptible to illness.

If you've been stressing for a while, you may experience any of the following physical symptoms:

• Headache • Fatigue • Difficulty sleeping • Difficulty focusing • Irritability • Upset stomach

When tension persists and is not adequately handled, it can lead to a variety of more severe health problems, such as:

• Down mood

• Hypertension (high blood pressure)

• Arrhythmia • Arterial hardening (atherosclerosis) • Pulmonary disease • Cardiac attack • Heartburn, ulcers, even irritable bowel syndrome • Upset stomach — cramps, constipation, and diarrhea • Weight gain or loss • Fertility issues

• Allergy or arthritis flare-ups • Cancer, eczema, or psoriasis skin issues

Pain management may have a significant impact on your fitness. Women with heart disease who participated in a stress management program lived longer, according to one report.

The Most Common Stressors

Stress is a natural and essential aspect of life to some degree. About the fact that stress is something that everyone goes through, what triggers it will vary from person to person.

Serious traffic congestion, for example, may make one person furious and overwhelmed, while another may turn up their music and consider it a minor nuisance. A dispute with a friend will last for the rest of the day for one person, although it can be quickly forgotten by another.

It's possible that the source of your stress is already something you're well aware of. However, given the importance of managing stress to reduce the negative impact it may have on your physical and mental health, it's worth considering the risk that other causes are at play as well. Make your stress-reduction strategy with them all in mind.

• Arguing with loved ones over finances • Being unable to open mail or answer the phone are both signs of financial tension.

• Worrying and feeling worried about finances • Feeling bad about wasting money on non-essentials

Long-term, financial stress causes anxiety, which can lead to high blood pressure, headaches, sore stomach, chest pain, insomnia, and a general feeling of ill health. Financial stress has also been attributed to depression, anxiety, skin disorders, diabetes, and arthritis.

Work on Coping with Financial Stress

According to the Centers for Disease Control and Prevention (CDC), Americans now spend 8% more hours at work than they did 20 years before, and 13% of the population works two jobs. At least 40% of respondents say their careers are difficult, and 26% say they are often stressed out. 2

Too much overtime, job instability, discontent with a job or profession, and problems with a manager and/or coworkers are all factors that may lead to job tension.

Putting your work ahead of anything else, whether you're concerned about a single assignment or felt poorly handled, may have a negative impact on multiple facets of your life, including intimate relationships and emotional and physical health.

Work stress is influenced by factors outside of the workplace, such as a person's psychological makeup, overall fitness, family life, and the amount of social support they have outside of work.

Physical and psychological symptoms of work-related stress include:

• Anxiety • Depression • Concentration or decision-making difficulties • Fatigue • Headache • Heart palpitations • Mood changes • Muscle stiffness and discomfort • Stomach issues

Some people can feel stressed and find it difficult to cope, which may have an effect on their behavior. People who are under a lot of pressure at work may develop: 4 • Less innovation and effort • Disinterest • Drops in job results • Increased sick days • Isolation • Lower patience and irritation levels • Problems with personal relationships

Stop bringing your work into your home.

Relationships with Others

We do have people in our life who cause us discomfort. It may be a close relative, a romantic partner, a friend, or a coworker. Toxic people exist in every aspect of our lives, and the tension we feel as a result of these interactions may have a negative impact on our physical and mental health.

In intimate relationships, there are many sources of tension, and when partners are continually under pressure, the relationship is at risk of failing.

The following are some of the most common partnership stressors:

5 • You and your spouse are too busy to spend time with each other and share commitments • Intimacy and intercourse have been scarce due to busyness, health issues, and a variety

of other causes • There is coercion or dominance in the partnership • You and your partner are not talking • You and/or partner are drinking too much alcohol and/or utilizing narcotics

Personal relationship stress symptoms are close to general stress symptoms, including physical well-being and sleep disorders, depression, and anxiety.

You may even find yourself avoiding or fighting with the person, or quickly annoyed by their presence.

Personal relationship tension is also linked to our interactions with strangers on social media sites like Facebook.

6 For example, social media encourages you to compare yourself to others, which may lead to feelings of inadequacy and tension. It also facilitates bullying.

What Effects Do Bad Relationships Have on Your Health?

Parenting is a challenging task.
Parents are often faced with juggling work, household responsibilities, and parenting children. Parenting tension is a product of these expectations.

High levels of parenting tension will lead to a parent being harsh, negative, and authoritarian towards their children. Parental tension may also have a negative impact on the consistency of the parent-child relationship. For example, if you don't have open contact with your child, he or she may not seek your counsel, or you and your child may sometimes disagree.

Being low-income, working long hours, single parenting, domestic or partnership tensions, or raising a child with a behavioral problem or developmental difficulty may all be sources of parenting stress.

Parents with children with behavioral problems and developmental disabilities are at the greatest risk of experiencing parental difficulties.

Busyness and Day-to-Day Life

Our everyday annoyances are our daily stressors. Misplacing keys, being late, and failing to carry a significant object with you while leaving the house are all examples. These are mostly small failures, but if they occur often enough, they may become a source of anxiety, negatively impacting physical and/or psychological health.

The burden of becoming overworked is becoming more regular. People are busier than ever these days, which brings a lot of tension to their lives.

Under certain situations, such as trying to perform a second career, busyness is unavoidable. Most times, it's out of remorse or a need to avoid disappointing someone. Owing to a lack of time, people may be unable to say "no" and therefore have little time for themselves, or they may neglect their own simple needs, such as eating well and exercising.

Suggestions on Changing Negative Thoughts

Anxiety in social and success circumstances is exacerbated by negative thoughts. Most social anxiety treatments have a component devoted to turning negative thinking processes into more helpful and optimistic ways of approaching scenarios.

Understanding how you think today (and the challenges that result) is the secret to overcoming your pessimistic feelings. From there, you can use tactics to alter your thoughts to make them have less impact. These measures are usually taken with the aid of a doctor, but they can also be used as part of a self-help strategy for managing social anxiety.

Recognize Your Thinking Style

Understanding how you think right now is one of the first steps toward altering your pessimistic thought habits. If you think of yourself as a total achievement or loss in any case, for example, you're speaking in "black-and-white" terms. Jumping to conclusions, catastrophizing, and overgeneralization are examples of pessimistic thought habits.

There are slight differences between unhelpful thought styles. However, they all include truth distortions and irrational approaches to circumstances and individuals.

Stop Negative Thoughts With These Techniques

1. Stopping Your Thoughts

When you find that negative thoughts or memories are beginning to creep into your mind, tell yourself, "No!" If you're home, consider saying it out loud, but it's still successful when spoken silently in your mind.

If you choose, you should use stronger words than "stop" (for example, "Get out of my mind!" or something a little more colorful). Images can be more effective than words for those who aren't motivated by words. When distracting thoughts start to surface, see a flashing red stop sign in your head.

Thinking stops may also be done in a more straightforward manner. You might, for example, use the old trick of splashing water in your face or just alter the way you think. Some people like counting down from 100 to one.

2. Affirmations that is positive

Positive affirmations may be used in a variety of ways. They could, for one, be used in the same way as thought-stopping tactics are. To put it another way, you might say an affirmation as soon as a negative thought crosses your mind.

For eg, if you're using the Law of Attraction to meet a new partner and you're saying to yourself, "I am a valuable, lovable individual who will find a great relationship," you might suggest,

"I am a valuable, lovable person who will find a great relationship."

Second, saying affirmations on a regular basis begins to reshape your mindset, making them a strong weapon even when you're not in a positive frame of mind. Make sure the affirmations are well-crafted, and when you recite them in front of the mirror, make eye contact with yourself.

3. Defining and Enforcing Boundaries

If you've been living with pessimistic thoughts for a long time, you can believe it's impossible to ask yourself to improve overnight. Also affirmations and mind-stopping exercises can appear to postpone negative thoughts in this case simply.

If this sounds like you, you should spend at least a couple of weeks enforcing limits around negative thoughts. The theory is that you set aside a set amount of time each week to stimulate your mind to entertain depressive thoughts and then contribute to forcibly stopping or resisting them over the rest of the week.

When you know you'll have time to think about these ideas, they'll feel less powerful and have less of a chance to take over your mind. Furthermore, several people discover that as they arrive at their designated time for contemplation of negative feelings, they are unable to think of something, which actually aids them in breaking their cycle.

4. Creating and Dismantling

If the negative feelings are associated with a powerful emotion such as anxiety, rage, or envy, consider writing them all down. Use a pen and paper to show all of the negative emotions. Then, as a sign of your dedication to going on, you can choose if you want to ruin this document. You might rip it up, mash it into a ball, burn it, or scribble all over it, for example.

Artistic endeavors may have a similar effect on those who aren't as focused on using language to describe themselves. You might, for example, sculpt or paint a picture of your negativity and then kill it (or change its shape).

This strategy aims to create a tangible image of your negativity so that you can banish it in a pleasing symbolic manner.

5. "For the Love of It"

When you find yourself beginning to descend into negativity, you should still attempt to reason with yourself. This approach entails coming up with a phrase that you should recite to understand that you have control of your bodily reactions and gradually improve that control.

Take a slow, cleansing breath and say something like, "Just because I've had some horrible relationships doesn't mean I have to do this to my body" or "Just because I've failed to find a decent career doesn't mean I'll never find one."

Tell "Now relax" after your chosen sentence (using the word "relax" as a prompt to exhale, releasing stress and negativity).

Negative Thoughts and How to Deal With Them

What is a pessimistic feeling, exactly?

Let's say a coworker or a grocery store clerk gives you a threatening glance. What will your reaction be? Will you ever let it go like water off a duck's back? Or would you take it personally and feel bad for yourself, if not outright enraged? You're getting pessimistic feelings if you turn little things into major problems that annoy you for days, weeks, or even months.

You can feel depressed and insecure as a result of negative thoughts. They detract from the enjoyment of life and may have a negative impact on your physical well-being. That is why it is important to understand how to cope with them.

What are certain strategies for dealing with suicidal thoughts?

One strategy for dealing with depressive feelings is to replace them with positive ones. Let's presume you've just discovered that you have a health issue. "My life will never be the same" or "This is the beginning of the end for me," you might tell yourself. It will almost certainly make you feel bad, and it will weaken your body right when you need it to be solid.

"This is going to be a struggle for a while," you might tell yourself, "but if I'm careful, I can learn to adapt and still enjoy my life," or

"This is a loss for me, but if I give myself time, I can heal." This type of thinking will make you feel more positive and optimistic. It also benefits the body.

If you have any pessimistic feelings running through your mind right now? (Sometimes it's difficult to tell.) Take a moment to listen to your mind and see if you can find something. Know that you are in control of what you tell yourself if you are telling yourself something that makes you feel terrible. But why not come up with something a little more upbeat?

They're "just thoughts," as they say. What really is the big deal? Your emotions will have a real impact on your wellbeing because of the mind-body relationship. You're asking your brain to create hormones that will lower your blood pressure and lower your risk of heart attack by telling yourself more positive things.

• Boost the immune system's ability to fight illness and disease.

• Help you feel less stressed by lowering your stress level.

• Make you feel happy and more hopeful about the future by preventing digestive pains, insomnia, and back pain.

What more would you do to boost your mood?
Bad feelings are often linked to the way you work day today. Here are a few things you can do right now to make you see the positive side of things:

• Pay attention to how you're feeling right now. Feel the pain if you're depressed. Just don't remind yourself that you've always been miserable and that you'll always be sad. Sadness fades away. Bad thinking will remain for a long time if you don't let it go.

• Tell someone close to you of your emotions. Everybody has depressive feelings now and then. Talking to someone else about it will help you put your feelings in perspective.

• Treat yourself to something good. Perhaps you will work less today and spend more time with your children. You might even look for something amusing.

• Take a moment to reflect on your blessings. There are so many things to be grateful for in and of our lives. What is one thing you value?

• Eat healthily. Good night's rest. Take part in activities. It's easier to feel better about yourself if you treat your body with respect.

• Create social ties. This is just a fancy way of saying "build the society you want." Spend time with your families and friends. Look for a church group that is a good fit for you. Join a sports team or a club. Take up a new pastime.

Anxiety-Inducing Factors

Anxiety disorders, which concern about 40 million people in the United States, are the most prevalent psychiatric illnesses.

Anxiety accompanying stress, worry, or fear can disrupt daily life, affecting work, school, and relationships. Anxiety can be crippling, particularly when panic attacks occur. Avoiding panic attacks and effectively treating this chronic and difficult disorder requires identifying anxiety causes and implementing coping mechanisms.

What Sets Anxiety in Motion?

Anxiety causes are specific events or acts that cause feelings of concern or terror. These causes will exacerbate symptoms to the point where a person has a panic attack. Panic attacks are brief bursts of intense and incapacitating terror. Internal causes, such as chronic medical problems, and external factors, such as traumatic life experiences, can also cause anxiety attacks.

Anxiety causes may include, but are not limited to:

• Caffeine: Caffeine causes nausea and exacerbates effects.

• Medical Conditions: Anxiety may be triggered by medical conditions such as cardiac problems, overactive thyroid function, and low blood sugar.

• Drugs: Anxiety can be triggered by prescription and over-the-counter medications such as hormonal birth control and cold medicines.

• Relationship Issues: Certain people may experience distress as a result of disagreements with their partner, parents, or other family members.

• Stress: Anxiety is often triggered by major life events such as graduation from college, the death of a loved one, divorce, or work loss.

• Workplace, school, or home conflicts: Conflicts between coworkers, classmates, or family members can cause severe stress and anxiety.

• Social Events: What causes social anxiety and the signs of anxiety attacks vary from person to person. Attending events, classes, or concerts may all be social anxiety causes.

• Finances: Worries about paying bills or putting money together for savings will cause a lot of tension and anxiety.

• Drug Abuse: Amphetamines and other stimulants can cause anxiety. Anxiety attacks are also believed to be triggered by alcohol.

• Public Speaking: For many people, performing in front of a crowd is terrifying.

• Sleep Pattern Interruptions: Anxiety is believed to be triggered by insufficient or disturbed sleep.

• Routine Changes: Changes of routine, such as starting a new career, delivering a kid, or starting college, can cause a lot of tension and anxiety.

Anxiety Triggers: How to Recognize Them

Anxiety sufferers may be unsure about how to recognize anxiety stimuli. While each person's anxiety causes are different, there are certain things that anxiety sufferers have in common. Identifying anxiety stimuli can assist a person in developing effective coping mechanisms to successfully treat their illness.

The below are some suggestions for identifying anxiety triggers:

• Write in a journal: Keeping a journal with your emotions is a perfect way to figure out what circumstances make you feel nervous. Additionally, writing down some good coping mechanisms may be useful for future reference.

• Recognize significant stressors: Marital problems, career changes or losses, pregnancy, or the death of a loved one may all trigger distress. Consider any recent stressors that may be contributing to your distress.

• Think about your previous experiences: Anxiety can be triggered by psychological stress. Remember how traumatic memories from the past can still be impacting you now.

• Speak with someone: When it comes to things that make you anxious, a trustworthy friend or family member may help. If you need more assistance, talk to a licensed therapist about working with the causes.

• Pay attention to the body: Keep track of what you're eating. Caffeine, sugary snacks, and alcohol all spike cortisol levels, which can make you feel anxious.

Identifying anxiety stimuli takes time and effort, but it may help a person develop effective coping strategies for treating their illness. A person can learn to deal with anxiety stimuli after they have been recognized.

Managing Anxiety Triggers

Anxiety can be difficult to treat as there are no established stimuli. However, regardless of a perceived cause, coping mechanisms may help to reduce anxiety.

• Schedule concern time to restrict its ability to overtake the day • Practice deep breathing exercises • Exercise consistently to relieve stress • Get enough sleep • Limit caffeine consumption • Practice calming practices such as yoga and meditation • Volunteer • Accept a lack of power • Maintain a normal routine to minimize confusion

Dealing with fear stimuli for certain people entails immediately facing an initiating situation. Joining a public speaking group, for example, can encourage someone to obtain enough confidence speaking in front of a group that it no longer causes them anxiety. Anxiety support groups or trained therapists may also assist an individual with learning how to deal with anxiety causes.

Anxiety effects can also be avoided by avoiding identified causes. Avoiding public places, abstaining from caffeine and alcohol, and breaking toxic relationships, for example, will also help to reduce anxiety attacks.

Anxiety and Panic Attacks Treatment

Managing life while dealing with anxiety and panic attacks can be difficult at times. Fortunately, fear can be managed with a combination of clinical assistance and self-care. Anxiety treatment choices include: • Medication: Anti-anxiety drugs such as benzodiazepines, antidepressants, and buspirone may help alleviate anxiety symptoms.

• Psychotherapy: Cognitive behavioral therapy (CBT) and occupational therapy are two therapeutic approaches that can help people understand anxious feelings and modify their behavior habits to deal with anxiety more effectively.

• Desensitization: Desensitization is the process of increasingly introducing a person to an anxiety trigger point until they become used to it. This method can be carried out by a certified mental health specialist who has been educated in the healthy desensitization of anxiety.

• Acupuncture: Acupuncture is a conventional Chinese procedure in which small needles are inserted through various pressure points on the body to achieve inner harmony.

• Therapy: When done correctly, meditation will help people understand the root of their fear and how to deal with it.

• Deep breathing exercises: Deep breathing exercises can help people prevent hyperventilation and feel calmer, which can help them avoid anxiety attacks.

• Yoga: Yoga will help you become more conscious by bringing your mind and body together by movement and stationary poses.

Anxiety-Inducing Circumstances

If you have a social anxiety disorder (SAD), many common circumstances are likely to make you feel anxious. Smells, sights, tastes, and feelings will all serve as triggers, both internal and external. Anxiety is often caused in people with a social anxiety disorder by particular social circumstances, such as speaking in public or meeting new people at a party.

Anxiety Triggers: An Overview

SAD is thought to be triggered by a combination of biological and environmental causes, including biology, brain chemistry, and traumatic life events or trauma. Anxiety stimuli, on the other hand, are people, environments, or things that make you feel anxious.

Anxiety stimuli are things that the brain has adapted or learned to interpret as threatening, causing acute anxiety symptoms like muscle stiffness, stomach distress, and shortness of breath.

Anxiety effects are not only disruptive and unpleasant, but they can also lead to behavioral changes. For example, when something makes you nervous, you're most likely to attempt to stop it to avoid the fear that comes with it. This may mean missing social situations, job opportunities, or even boring things like going to the grocery store for people with SAD.

The first step in dealing with anxiety triggers is to recognize them so that you can learn how to deal with them.

Anxiety Triggers That Are Common

Although any social or performance condition has the ability to elicit social anxiety, there are a few common causes for people who suffer from social anxiety. You could have one or more reasons, which is why figuring out what they are will help you prevent or better deal with your social anxiety disorder.

Keep a diary or use an anxiety app to keep track of the social interactions that cause you anxiety.

Athletic events, instrumental shows, and public speaking are also examples of performances. People with SAD who are afraid of these circumstances often feel that their discomfort prevents them from functioning to their full potential. Fears of public speaking will also prevent you from progressing with your profession.

What It's Like to Work as a Social Anxiety Disordered Employee

Meeting New People and Attending Parties

A room full of people is one of the most common causes of social anxiety. If you have SAD, meeting new people or going to a party where you don't know anybody will be difficult.

Talking For Nothing

Although small talk comes naturally to some people, those with SAD can find it difficult to engage in this form of conversation. Small talk can make you nervous when you're afraid of saying something dumb or making a mistake. It may increase your anxiety if the outsider or acquaintance with whom you are trying to strike up a conversation is an authority figure, such as a teacher, educator, or employer.

The 10 Best and Worst Small Talk Conversation Topics

Reading and writing

If you suffer from SAD, you may be afraid of writing in front of someone. This concern comes from the fact that someone would see your hands trembling when you type. Any people with SAD have a fear of reading aloud in front of others in addition to a fear of writing.

Expressing your point of view

Do you fear expressing your point of view? Do you agree with what other people think, even though you don't agree with them? People with SAD are also unable to express their feelings for fear of being judged.

When you're eating in Front of Everyone

Any people with SAD have an irrational fear of eating in public, which can be caused by a number of scenarios, foods, and dining partners. They may be fearful of spilling a drink or eating in front of authority figures, or of someone seeing their shaking hands when eating.

Making Use of Public Restrooms

The avoidance of using public toilets without medical need is known as paruresis, also known as aerophobia, shy kidney, shy bladder, or bashful bladder syndrome (BBS). For certain people with SAD, it may be crippling, making travel, social obligations, and professional responsibilities impossible.

The Real Reason You Hate Using Public Restrooms

Obtaining Assistance

Feelings of social anxiety may be triggered by a number of circumstances. If the fear of these situations is interfering with your normal life and you have not found treatment, it is important that you see a mental health specialist.

Treatments for SAD have included cognitive behavioral therapy (CBT), which includes exposure therapy, cognitive restructuring, and social skills instruction, as well as medicine.

The below are some of the most common drugs used to combat social anxiety:

Paxil CR (paroxetine), Zoloft (sertraline), Luvox CR (fluvoxamine), Celexa (citalopram), Lexapro (escitalopram), Prozac (fluoxetine) are examples of selective serotonin reuptake inhibitors (SSRIs) (fluoxetine)

• Effexor XR (venlafaxine), Cymbalta (duloxetine), and Pristiq are SNRIs (serotonin-norepinephrine reuptake inhibitors) (desvenlafaxine)

Nardil (phenelzine), Parnate (tranylcypromine), and Marplan are monoamine oxidase inhibitors (MAOIs) (isocarboxazid)

• Benzodiazepines: Ativan (lorazepam), Valium (diazepam), Xanax (alprazolam), Klonopin (klonopin) • Beta Blockers: Inderal (propranolol), Tenormin (atenolol) (clonazepam)

Treatments for Social Anxiety Disorder that Work

Anxiety Triggers and How to Deal With Them

If you suffer from mild to moderate social anxiety, self-help exercises such as mindfulness (visualization, deep breathing, and gradual muscle relaxation) and self-talk (challenging pessimistic thoughts) will help you get through the day.

Many individuals with social anxiety disorder lack assertiveness, and learning how to express their desires in a relaxed and calming manner will help. Learning to be more confident will make it possible to request any accommodations at work or school that will help you cope with your fear, such as a microphone or a pitcher of water whenever you have a speech or presentation to deliver.

Dealing with anxiety stimuli necessitates preparation as well. For example, before going to a party, set a time limit for yourself or write a checklist to plan for some small talk on a first date.

Most notably, you can support yourself by being gentle with yourself while you work to recognize your personal causes and figure out how to avoid them from interfering with your everyday life.

Anxiety Triggers and How to Recognize Them

A catalyst is an event that causes a recall, flashback, heart attack, anxiety attack, or other reaction. Physical or emotional triggers are common, and they are normally very personal; different factors cause different individuals. You may start avoiding circumstances and triggers that she or he believes caused the flashback.

Any causes are apparent, such as meeting a parent that has been violent in the past, visiting a spot that brings back painful feelings, or chasing an old flame on Facebook (hands up if you've done this). However, our causes aren't always clear. Learning how to control symptoms is just part of the treatment for anxiety. It also entails recognizing and confronting stimuli in order to reduce, or at the very least, the impact of the trigger on us.

So, how can you figure out what the reasons are?

• What are you eating right now? Take note about how you respond to caffeine, alcohol, sugar, or other mind-altering drugs, as they can all cause anxiety or raise cortisol levels (which, in turn, can cause anxiety!). There are so many potential triggers!!).

• Identify key sources of tension in your life: Big life stressors or life transitions can also trigger anxiety. Workplace stress or job changes (including loss of employment), pregnancy or childbirth, violence, trauma, or abuse, or the death of a loved one are all common triggers. Consider any life stressors you've faced and how they've influenced or triggered your anxiety.

• Think back on previous experiences: Anxiety can sometimes arise as a result of a frightening or traumatic event. Your fear causes could be linked to a traumatic encounter you've had in the past. Consider some negative encounters you've had and how they've influenced you; are you still affected?

• Keep a journal of your depressive symptoms: When you're feeling nervous, write down your feelings and how you respond to them. Begin with the condition that you know makes you nervous, such as giving a presentation or taking an exam. What ideas come to mind? What are the strategies for dealing with them? When you're close or in the middle of a crisis, how do you handle it? After that, how do you feel? This proved to be the most successful method for identifying my causes.

• Speak with someone: Your friends and relatives will be able to assist you. Inquire to those nearest to you if they find something that makes you anxious. People who know you best will also supply you with useful information.

• How do you cope with your fear until you've found out what's behind it?

When we have a bad reaction to a stimulus (for example, getting a heart attack when your employer calls you for a meeting), our brain (or more accurately, the amygdala, or "fear center") is associating the trigger (your boss) with a negative experience from the past (you were fired from your past employment). We can't even regulate the pain or anxiety caused by the negative case. The stimulus causes us to feel "learned" apprehension or distress, which we will "unlearn" by replacing it with new experiences.

Triggers can be difficult to manage. Of anxiety cause would have its own therapy options, and the best way to avoid this anxiety causes is to "unlearn" and then "re-learn" anxiety coping mechanisms. The below are few examples of treatments:

• Trigger Prevention: One of the simplest solutions is to actually live a life that prioritizes trigger avoidance. Fears over fitness can be reduced by living a healthy lifestyle that includes exercise. Avoiding television will help you feel less anxious in everyday situations. There are several approaches to overcome individual fears in order to minimize the risk of anxiety being triggered. We can't, though, stop any of our causes, such as our supervisor. It's neither practical nor safe, so it's best to figure out what's behind the causes and deal with them. Don't run away from reality.

• Trigger Desensitization: You might also attempt desensitization. It's a word for intentionally "activating" a stimulus so many times that it no longer triggers fear. If you feel anxious when you have a certain idea, for example, repeat the thought until it no longer induces anxiety. The mind is very adaptable, and one of the reasons emotions and objects create anxiety is that the mind battles them instead of being used to them. However, this did not fit in my experience. It only made matters harder when I started dwelling on my anxiety and was constantly stuck in a spiral of depressive thinking — all triggered by my trigger (s).

• Acknowledgement of Anxiety Triggers: When you feel an anxiety trigger, strive to become aware of the fact that your anxiety level rises. Check to see if it's rational, and pay attention to the symptoms. Stopping the stimulus from cascading into worse fear is a common way to relieve anxiety. This level of mindfulness can be difficult to master, but it can be extremely beneficial.

• See a therapist: If your anxiety is interfering with your daily life, be honest. Speak with a therapist who can help you understand your fear, recognize your causes, and develop a recovery plan. It won't be simple (or cheap), but it has the potential to transform your life.

CLEAN UP YOUR MIND

For less tension and calmer, try these 24 deliberate ways to clear a cluttered mind.

1. Workout on a regular basis

Exercise not only benefits our bodies, but it also provides us with time to think. It improves our sleep, promotes a healthier appetite, and activates feel-good chemicals that are beneficial to both our bodies and minds. Choose an activity that you love, that blends with your lifestyle, and that you can maintain on a regular basis.

2. Arrange your to-do list in order of importance.

Don't overburden your to-do list to the point where you accomplish nothing but stress yourself out. Choose only a few things to do each day, say three, and make sure you complete them. If you need to get stuff out of your head and into paper, you should still keep a different list to apply to for tomorrow (always helpful for decluttering your mind).

3. Develop a mindfulness practice.

The desire to be now, to relax in the here and now, completely committed to whatever we're doing at the time, is known as mindfulness. Maintain your attention on a single goal and complete it to the best of your abilities. It doesn't matter whether you're eating cookies or planning for a presentation at work! "Wherever you are, be all there," Jim Elliot says.

4. Do not squander your time.

Perhaps the most valuable resource you have is your leisure. I'm not saying you have to be ambitious and do tasks every second of the day; we all need downtime to unwind. Consider how you spend your time during the day to see if some of these classic time-wasters come to mind. Prioritize what matters most, learn to be reliable and successful, and make the most of the time you do have.

5. Make time for yourself.

Don't undervalue the importance of taking care of yourself and making time for yourself. That's your day to do whatever you want, from reading to practicing karate. I'm sure you spend a lot of your time doing stuff for other people, but set aside some time per day to do something just for you.

6. Make specific objectives.

Make a list of priorities to help you find meaning and focus on your life. It's fine to fly by the seat of your pants or to be sheltered by the heavy winds of life now and then. However, if you want things to happen in your life and build a healthy life for you and your family, you'll actually benefit from setting a few targets and making a strategy to accomplish them. "A mission without a roadmap is just a wish," said Antoine de Saint-Exupéry.

7. Develop good habits

Develop everyday routines that are both physically and mentally beneficial to you. Check your eating habits, choose nutritious foods and diets, set aside time for self-improvement and learning new skills, form mutually beneficial relationships, and don't go to bed too late and wonder why you hit the snooze button in the morning! For more tips, look at these good behaviors to incorporate into your everyday routine.

8. Get enough rest.

Sleep is essential for your body to recharge and rejuvenate. You put many demands on your body every day, so treat it well and provide it with what it needs, such as a structured evening routine and plenty of sleep.

9. Keep the screen time to a minimum.

Don't let yourself get engrossed in a computer screen, television, or another gadget for an extended period of time without keeping track of how long you've been using it. Many of us depend on screens for jobs, but find other ways to unwind in our spare time. Pick up a hobby, start baking, read books, listen to podcasts, play board games... Switch off the glare and the annoying pings and warnings. Instead of focusing on social media, focus on the surroundings.

10. Maintaining a healthy work-life balance

If far as possible, limit the number of hours you travel and find ways to reconcile work and home life. Time for your family, time for your interests, and time for you. They're all crucial. Have an eye out for signs that the work-life balance is off, and take action before it takes you down.

11. Make time to meditate.

Meditation requires time, and I must confess that I am not very good at it! Persistence, however, pays off, and I've discovered that guided meditations available on the internet are extremely helpful in getting me in the right state of mind. If you want to learn more, go to Headspace.com.

12. Make sure the schedule isn't too full.

Have an eye on your calendar, and if everything becomes too hectic and you don't have time to breathe, don't be scared to cancel or delay events. Create spare time to relieve stress, giving yourself some wiggle room for emergencies, doing something on the spur of the moment, and being late for meetings, and just enjoy doing whatever you want once in a while.

13. Don't bother about multitasking.

Multitasking is detrimental to the brain. We lose attention and concentration every time we turn from one task to another. If far as possible, focus on one task at a time to complete it before moving on to the next. Other time management advice can be found in my article.

14. Brainstorming

Get your ideas out of your mind and onto paper, where you can see them plainly, prioritize them, and take action. Swirling, jumbled emotions that simply cloud your mind are useless to you. Check out my essay on how to declutter your mind by brain-dumping.

15. Work on unhealthy thinking habits.

Negative thought processes may be perplexing and harmful. Take action to change your attitude and address unhelpful habits of behavior and perception, such as perfectionism and procrastination.

16. Keep a journal

Writing down your feelings on paper can be a calming and cathartic means of exploring both positive and negative emotions. Check out this article for some self-discovery journal prompts.

17. How do you take care of yourself?

Self-care, in whatever form it takes for you, should be done on a daily basis. Check out my regular self-care tips, inspiration, and support to help you put yourself first for a change!

18. Organize your house

Without mentioning decluttering, no post of mine will be final! There are several reasons to declutter your home, build more space, make it easier to care for your home, and provide yourself with more time, resources, and independence to care for yourself!

19. Make fewer decisions

Every day, the average adult makes about 35,000 choices! To free up more precious mental resources, reduce the number of choices you make each day. To make it easier to choose what to eat and wear each day, try meal prep or decluttering your closet. That's a lot of decisions taken care of!

20. Take on the beauty of nature

Nature has such a soothing effect. Get as much time as possible outside, looking at the leaves and flowers, feeling the breeze and warmth on your face, and inhaling the fresh air.

21. Recognize the symptoms of a cluttered mind

Consider how you feel when your mind is jumbled. Do you find yourself perplexed or distracted? Is it impossible for you to unwind, rest, or sleep? Is it tough for you to make decisions or keep your attention on the job at hand? Are you irritable, teary-eyed, or enraged? Knowing the symptoms will alert you to the fact that your mind is cluttered and in need of some clarity.

22. Let go of the past.

"Don't mind the little stuff," says Richard Carlson. Pick your fights, ignore the unimportant, and concentrate on the big picture. The little irritations of today will most likely be overlooked by tomorrow.

23. Make a list of everything.

From filling your head with insignificant information about your everyday life. Instead of putting your reminders, assignments, and random ideas in your memory, keep a diary handy and jot them down.

Using your phone's notes or Trello (a fantastic piece of software that's simple to use and convenient to keep notes on). I'm not an affiliate, but I'm a huge fan!

24. Learn to switch off the lights at night.

Learning to declutter your mind at night can be beneficial, but it takes time and planning. Create a relaxing evening routine and a tranquil bedroom to aid in your physical and mental relaxation.

How to Discover Your Passion and Live a Life That Is More Fulfilling

If you could only do one thing to change your life, I would strongly advise you to pursue something you are passionate about and make a living at it. Finding your love may not be as easy as it seems, but it is well worth the effort.

You should consider searching for a new career whether you hate going to work, are chronically losing inspiration, or find what you're doing boring and tedious.

Staying in your present career will not only keep you trapped and depressed, but it will also prevent you from reaching your full potential in life.

Instead, do this:

You get out of bed early in the morning, eager to get to work. You can work more hours than the average worker, but you don't find it tough because your work hours fly by.

You are always in a state of mind known as "flow," in which you lose track of time and the outside world, completely immersed in the job at hand. Job isn't what many people think about when they think of work; it's something enjoyable, fascinating, and thrilling. It's not a "work," but rather a love that contributes to a happy life.

If you have a career that you dread or even despise, this would seem like a pipe dream. And such a thing would never be possible if you never put in the initiative to discover what you are curious about.

It is, therefore, not only a chance, but a likelihood, if you venture to inquire, "How do I find my passion?" imagine the possibilities, and really look for what you love.

How do you go about learning how to discover your life's passion? Here are a few recommendations:

1. Do you already have a passion for something?
Do you have a hobby or a pastime that you enjoyed as a kid but never saw as a career option?

There's definitely a way for you to make a living doing things you like, whether it's reading comic books, collecting something, or designing or constructing something. Open a comic book store or an online comic book site.

You're already ahead of the curve if you have a passion for something. Now all you have to do is look at how you can profit from it.

2. Figure out what you spend hours reading about. When I get really excited about something, I'll read about it for hours. I'll go out and buy some books and magazines. I'll spend days searching the web for more details.

There could be a few options here for you, and they're all viable career paths. Don't shut your eyes off of these ideas. Examine them until you're satisfied, as this will assist you in getting started while you learn how to find your passion.

3. Have a brainstorming session
If you're wondering how to find my passion and nothing comes to mind right away, take out a piece of paper and start jotting down ideas. It isn't necessary for this to be a well-organized list.

It may simply be a piece of paper with scribbles or doodles on it. All of this will come in handy at some point.

4. Consult with others

There are probably people in your life that you respect, and there are aspects of their personalities that you wish to emulate. If at all necessary, approach them and select their brain. Examine how they got to where they are now and why they believe they've found their calling.

The more options you discover, the more likely you are to learn how to discover your interest in the long term. This may mean that you waste your spare time chatting to friends and relatives, colleagues, or even strangers.

5. Hold off on quitting the job just yet.

Don't just hand in your resignation tomorrow if you feel your calling, your passion. It's best to keep your current position while you investigate your options.

It's much cooler if you can do your hobby as a side job and earn money for a few months or a year. It allows you to save money (which you'll use if you go into business for yourself) while also allowing you to practice the skills you'll need.

6. First, give it a shot.

When you're trying to figure out how to find your passion, it's best to put your new project to the test before committing to it as a career. At first, do it as a hobby or a side job and see if it's really your true calling.

You can be enthusiastic about it for a few days, but if you are passionate about it for at least a few months is where the rubber hits the road.

You've hopefully found it if you pass this exam.

7. Do as much research as you can

Learn as much as you can in your passion. You could have already been doing this if this has been a long-time hobby of yours. In either case, do further analysis. Read any website you can find on the subject and invest in the best books available.

Find other people who do what you want to do for a living in your town or on the Internet and question them about it.

How much do they get, and what kind of schooling and preparation did they require? What abilities are needed, and how did they develop? What suggestions do they have for you?

You'll frequently find that people are eager to provide advice.

8. Practice, practice, practice, and then practice some more.

If you're close to figuring out how to find your passion, don't go into it with a beginner's skill set. You must have technical qualifications if you wish to make money—to be a professional.

Get very good at your future job, and you'll be able to make a lot of money. Train for hours on end to learn to concentrate; if it's something you like, the practice can be enjoyable.

9. Never Give Up Trying

It's true that you won't discover your passion right away. You will, though, lose if you give up after a few days. Keep searching, even though it takes months, and you'll finally find it.

Maybe you believed you'd realized your calling, only to find after a few months that it wasn't for you. Restart your quest for a new love. There's a good chance you'll have more than one love in your lifetime, so take advantage of them all.

Have you discovered your calling but haven't been able to make a living from it? Continue to try and try before you excel. Giving up too much is a sure way to lose and success does not come easily.

The Make It Happen Handbook will provide you with a good action plan to help you turn your ambition into a job if you need it. Take a look at the handbook and start living your dream!

Remember that this will take a lot of time and effort, but it will be the greatest investment you've ever made. If you take the time to learn how to find your passion, you will find that your days are more rewarding and that you are happier and well-adjusted in the long run.

When you live your passion, amazing things happen.

Have you ever considered how wonderful your life would be if you were able to practice your passion every day? It just feels like yesterday that you were the boy who wanted to be an astronaut, a pilot, or an inventor. It feels like just yesterday that you graduated from high school, got your first job, and plotted your career path.

Then the unforeseen occurred... you matured.

What exactly does it mean to mature? And why does it seem that "growing up" entails giving up your hopes and passions?

Although culture will have you think that following your dreams is reckless and childish, we'll concentrate on 14 cool things that happen when you do.

1. Increased Self-Assuredness

Everyone needs to be respected for who they are, according to a little-known fact. However, not everyone is at ease voicing them. You will be more at ease sharing yourself if you disregard other people's views and live your passion.

When you're not pursuing your passion, you're also living a life you think is reasonable to others. When you give in to the demands of society, peers, and family, your confidence will suffer. This is mainly due to the fact that you are pushing yourself to do something that you dislike.

There is definitely a valid explanation for this, and your success will suffer as a result of not operating within your abilities and desires.

2. Stress Reduction

Adults' primary cause of stress is work, which is linked to "increased rates of heart disease, hypertension, and other illnesses."

Let me begin by dispelling the myth that all tension is harmful. And those who pursue their passions and those who do not will be stressed. The kind of tension you encounter makes a difference.

Many that follow their passion have an innate drive that lets them maintain a sense of order in their lives. As a consequence, they will most likely face a variety of difficult scenarios. Consider the following scenario: you have three critical tasks due on the same day. As a result, you'll be stressed for the rest of the day.

Many who are not pursuing their passion are likely to dislike their jobs and find them exhausting on a daily basis. They are stressed by the act of waking up, dressing, and driving to work. They hate Mondays and look forward to Fridays.

3. Workplace Satisfaction

Nothing is more draining than "working to live," as we said earlier. You're trapped and you have bills to cover and your career is the only way to pay them.

And if your passion is a little hazy, the importance of enjoying what you do cannot be overstated.

You will feel happy at work if you pursue your passion. When living, you won't have the need to listen to podcasts or audiobooks (trying to fill that unfulfilled void). Instead of planning to live your passion, you will have the pleasure of doing so. There is nothing more satisfying than fulfilling your destiny.

4. Work-Life Balance Mastery

It's been said that if you follow your passion, you won't need a work-life balance. Work-life balance is only necessary when the work is exhausting, according to the premise.

Your life is in perpetual flux as you are chasing your passion. Since you can do it for free, your work does not feel like a career.

Imagine hoping you should be employed and you are passionate about what you do. When you pursue your passion that is precisely what will happen.

5. Less regrets as you get older

In the end, most people would lament the things they did not do more than the things they did.

Consider how different your life would be if you followed all of your desires and interests. Consider what you'd say if you bumped into another person and had to justify why you didn't follow your dream. When it's all but too late, this is the real-life conversation that most people are having.

Take a chance and put your money on yourself. And if it does not turn out the way you had hoped, you would be a better person for it.

6. Personal Development

Because of the mystery surrounding their love, most people do not practice their passion. You might be unsure of your potential to excel financially, mentally, or emotionally.

You are often right with your assumptions. This isn't to say that you can embrace truth and do nothing to change it. Instead, devote some time to honing the skills needed to pursue your passion.

If you ever want to be an astronaut, you might choose a career as a space scientist. If you ever want to be a pilot, you should train and get your pilot's license.

Make a list of the qualities you'll need to pursue your passion, and then take the necessary steps to achieve them.

Positive Attraction is number seven.

You may be concerned that your zeal will not be well received by anyone. The problem with leading a less-than-authentic life is that you can draw the wrong people.

You will meet like-minded people if you live your life and pursue your interests.

To be frank, as you pursue your passion, you will almost certainly irritate certain people. People dislike change, and as you change, the relationships will change as well.

But don't let this get in the way of your progress. Your ability to accomplish your goal is dependent on your desire to follow the values that will help you achieve it.

8. Get outside of your comfort zone

Do not slip into the pit of thinking that following your passion requires you to give up everything. These forms of restrictive values prevent most people from even continuing their path to improve their lives.

In reality, you don't have to throw anything away to start over. Here's why.

Allow you to gradually get outside of your comfort zone and explore new experiences. You will continue to enjoy your existing life, while seeking new experiences on the side.

When you get more relaxed with your ability to live your passion, you can eventually shift more time into it. Before you know it, you will be all-in and live your life to the fullest.

9. Give Thanks

It is true that you should and should be thankful all the time. In your life, there is still much to be thankful for. And if you have a flat tire on your way home from work, at least you have a car.

Similarly, you should be grateful for your work at all times. Yet, there is no doubt that you would be more grateful if you are doing something you are excited about every day. You might realistically find yourself eager to get up every morning because you know it is another day to fulfill your life's mission.

10. Reconnect with the Inner-Self

There was a moment when you were free. You feel like you could do something and anything was possible.

When you start living your passion, you are most definitely reconnecting with things you enjoyed as a kid. By having a break and remembering the things you cherished before society told you what to love, you are discovering a missing piece of yourself.

Revisit your childhood joys and take stock of what you enjoyed doing. Like me, you can find that you enjoy putting puzzles together. This could speak on your intellectual nature and make you understand why you are so curious about bringing ideas together and solving problems.

Whatever it may be, take a moment to rediscover the "real you" that was forced to "grow up".

11. Kinder Person

Your enthusiasm is most definitely going to help a lot of people. There is something wrong with the environment that you think you can hopefully fix. Although more people will live their dream, there is no chance the world will be a happier place.

There is a harmony and pleasure that you will experience when you are enjoying your passion, and that will rub off on your relationships with others. You may have heard the saying, "hurt people, hurt people". This means that the person who is bad at your work is most likely struggling with something of their own life.

When you fulfill your passion, you are fulfilled and at one with the world, and you will be kinder to everyone.

12. Unleash Your Creativity

The thing about living a life devoid of your passion is that you are most likely living the widely walked course. Security in life is always the lack of imagination.

When you abandon the road of least resistance and start to live your passion, you must unleash your imagination to succeed. You are going to be venturing into uncharted waters in your life and that can be overwhelming. So that is when the magic occurs.

When you find yourself face to face with a challenge logged between you and your passion, you need to believe in yourself that you can succeed.

13. Change the Narrative

You have an invisible voice that is reminding you who you are, what you should do, and what you deserve. Often you have split thoughts in finding your passion.Onn the one side, you are thankful for the life you have and happy with what it means. Or you have a burning need to follow your dream and take a chance.

By knowing the crippling narrative you are asking yourself (I am not good enough, I should be satisfied with the work I have now, etc.), you would be best able to adjust your narrative.

Your current story can be grounded in the awareness that you should fulfill your passion without that meaning you are ungrateful or unappreciative of the life you have now.

14. Conquer Your Fears

Fear leads to procrastination and procrastination leads to the demise of the ability to fulfill your passion.

Avoid the desire to rationalize leaving things the way they are until you get more experience, more opportunity, and more control. There will always be more than might be easier. If you give in to your worries, they can only begin to rise.

By living your passion, you would have set your fears in their place. Remember, it is okay to be scared, it is not okay to cause the fear to stall your efforts.

What Is Passion and What It Does To Have Passion

How to Know What You Are Passionate About?

Finding what you are curious about is a journey in itself. Don't get disappointed if you don't feel like you know yet. Keep trying new ideas. It will come even though you have to create it. If you find your love, or find yourself hot on its trail, don't give it up.

What if you know what you have a love for so you don't do something about it? This is the biggest challenge with zeal. You may have all the enthusiasm in the world for anything but if you never do something about it, the passion is pointless.

Maybe you work a decent job that pays all the bills but it doesn't encourage you to pursue your passion fully. You're scared of what will happen if you shake it up. Yes, the transition is frightening, but it's not until we leave our comfort zone that we discover what we've been missing out on.

You're the author of your life. Don't settle for the bare minimum only because it's working out right now.

You will never know what you're really capable of until you press yourself.

But even as you seek your passion, you will find yourself tripped up by mistakes and other hurdles. You can't let it get to you. It happens to anyone in the journey of chasing their passion. Abe Lincoln has a deep enthusiasm for creating a great nation. Do you think he let a few mistakes deter him from that? Don't let challenges get you down.

What about Passion for People?

The definition of emotion also extends to women. Don't slip into the traditional pit of believing you love someone and not doing anything about it. Ask yourself, is giving away my ego worth it to sustain a relationship? What about being unselfish and wasting your time or comfort? If you can't do that, it's either not true love, or you ought to start making adjustments.

Often, I think we ought to remind ourselves who we love and behave accordingly. It's tempting to let family bonds weaken out of pride. Of course, you say you love your family, but when your brother is in the school play, and you hate shows, do you go?

The same refers to romantic relationships. Do you just love them when it's easy? Real love requires sacrifice and effort. You push through the difficult times because you love them and you understand that every passion pursued will have bumps in the road. Unfortunately, many people don't understand what it means to have a passion for someone. This is why divorce rates are so high and families are often torn apart by hurt feelings and unnecessary drama.

Following any passion takes vulnerability and work. But I promise in the end, the outcome of such efforts will be the most fulfilling in your life.

Chapter 3 How to stop Overthinking? Best ways to avoid it?

Overthinking Disorder - What is it?

Overthinking Disorder doesn't exist, on the contrary there are many different kinds of anxiety disorders where an individual involves in overthinking or reflection, but there is no disorder. Your quality of life can be interfered when an individual cannot stop worrying and obsessing over things.

The conditions that cause overthinking are those mental health diagnoses where a person can't stop your brain from rumination like PTSD, trauma, phobias, agoraphobia, panic disorder, separation anxiety disorder, substance-induced anxiety disorders, selective mutism, social anxiety disorder or it could probably be a symptom of some other disease.

When it comes to anxiety disorders, many of them have to overthink as a symptom. For example, people with panic disorder might ruminate and overthink when they are going to have a panic attack again. They fixated on something that could trigger their attack. They are not only anxious, they also suffer meta-anxiety, which is anxiety about being anxious. They feel the panic attack more enormous because they overthink about it.

Overthinking is common. You don't have to suffer an anxiety disorder to involve in constant rumination, it's part of the human condition. Sometimes you may be overly concerned with what you said or did to somebody. You may be worried about suffering at school or work. You might be worry about how others perceive you. These are different situations that might involve in overthinking.

Overthinking is omnipresent, but there's a treatment for the condition. Many people suffer from worrying and obsessing about things that they cannot control. Cognitive Behavior Therapy (CBT) is a common treatment for this type of anxiety; it helps people challenge their negative or annoying thoughts and change their thinking into positive, productive ones. Someone with overthinking can benefits in getting therapy or counseling for anxiety. You can work with a therapist in your local area, or with one of the trained mental health professionals here at Better Help. A perfect place to work on anxiety and start learning coping skills to manage it is online counseling.

Excessive consideration
Many people are comfortable with the term anxiety disorder (and millions of Americans suffer from it on a daily basis), but we sometimes forget one of the most common symptoms of anxiety disorders: overthinking.

Overthinking is described as ruminating or obsessing about something. Many people can believe they are overthinkers after hearing this term. Who hasn't seen a day when they haven't overthought something? We wonder if we're making the right decisions about everything from our children's well-being to our family's safety and security, from little things like choosing the shortest path on our daily commute to choosing the right restaurant for dinner. But that's to be anticipated. Worrying and overthinking are normal occurrences.

Overthinking, on the other hand, may have negative behavioral and emotional consequences. Excessive thoughts about something that triggers distress, tension, terror, or dread can be considered overthinking in the context of an anxiety disorder. It's not about stressing too hard about something; it's obsessing about something to the point that it interferes with one's ability to work.

When you doubt or stress about yourself, your life, your work, your friends, or something else, because you don't have an overthinking problem, whatever you're pondering about bothers you for a bit, so you go about your day. You fret from time to time, but you don't ruminate endlessly. You don't think that your worry is messing with your other activities. However, when a person suffers from overthinking as a result of an anxiety disorder, stress is what they can think about, and they're still worried about something, even though they don't obsess about it all the time.

If you assume you have anxiety-related overthinking, you may have seen one or more of the following situations:

- Difficulty following through with and contributing to a conversation when you go through potential responses or statements over and over before the conversation has either ended or the window of opportunity for speaking has passed - Constantly comparing yourself to someone and how you compare to them - Focusing on worst-case scenarios involving yourself or others you care for

- An inability to control the rushing impulses, fears, or emotions Overthinking affects no two people in the same way. Many, who do, though, will find that their failure to suppress negative feelings and impulses successfully has a negative impact on their quality of life. Since their mind spends a vast amount of time and attention on single lines of thinking, it may find it more difficult to socialize, pursue hobbies, or be efficient at work. There's a feeling like they don't have enough control of their minds or feelings, which can be very harmful to one's mental health.

Overthinking makes it impossible to make or keep friends and you fail to communicate when something is wrong or you can communicate overly. It's difficult to speak to them because you're worried about what you'll hear, or to do something with them because you're worried about how you'll respond or what could happen. Overthinkers can find it difficult to carry on basic discussions or engage in a regular setting. Even going to the pharmacy or to an appointment can be daunting for them.

The reality is that overthinking has an effect on every aspect of your life. It will have an effect on how you communicate with people, your social life, and your personal life. That means it can begin to wear you down, as well as the relationships you have with those around you. Overthinking will lead to a slew of issues in your life.

How to Refrain from Overthinking
"Stop second-guessing yourself!"

You've already seen this before, and it's not that helpful. You can't just turn a knob to avoid overthinking. In reality, being advised to avoid overthinking sometimes causes you to overthink stuff. It's a never-ending loop.

Essentially, training your brain to not overthink is a long journey that you must go through. Let's take a look at some of the most important causes of overthinking and how to avoid them.

Overthinking Insomnia
When you can't sleep, your mind races and you might have obsessive thoughts about sleeping. Overthinking also occurs as a result of insomnia and lasts the next day. Your brain may be less concentrated and you may feel drained. You may be

having gloomy and obsessive feelings about the inability to sleep.

For a cause, insomnia is referred to as a vicious loop. It's difficult to resist overthinking about not sleeping until you've got it. When you're having trouble sleeping, there are a few things you can do to help.

• Apps for meditation and mindfulness. These assist you with living in the current moment, removing any distracting feelings or feelings. Mindfulness can not only prepare the brain, but it can also help you relax and sleep well.

• If you can't sleep, get out of bed. It can seem difficult to fall asleep in bed if you're having trouble falling asleep. Your subconscious correlates restlessness with your brain. Get out there to do something enjoyable. Spend less time on social media and more time doing something relaxing. Instead, try to unwind.

• Accept that you need not perish as a result of your lack of sleep. If your fear and anxiety can keep you awake at night, most cases are just temporary. Though chronic sleep deprivation wreaks havoc on your wellbeing, obsessing about a single bout of insomnia will exacerbate the issue. It's time to see a doctor or psychiatrist if the condition continues.

Making a Decision

Another explanation people overthink is that they are making a decision. It's not uncommon for a major decision to be made. Most times, the decision is made on a frivolous matter, such as which restaurant to choose.

Although you can consider your options, overthinking them simply wastes time, especially if a large number of people are waiting for you to make a decision. Here's how to actually get over the fear of making decisions.

•Set a time limit on yourself when making decisions. This time period should not have to be so limited that you feel hurried, but it should be sufficient to save you from overthinking.

•Many people, especially major decision-makers, plan their thought hours and end up wasting time in the process. Overthinking fear can be avoided by setting aside specific moments to consider.

•Mindfulness and staying in the current moment can improve here, as well. The focus should be on the logic behind the decision, not on any irrational concerns you might have.

•You may be able to change your mind about a decision under certain circumstances. It will be easier to make a decision until you realize this.

Overthinking and Anxiety

Overthinking is a symptom of many psychiatric disorders, and there is a clear connection between fear and overthinking. Anxious people are just in the actual moment.

Parts of the brain are constantly concerned with what will happen next, and fear and overthinking will make it difficult to leave the house.

When you're nervous brain tells you no, here's how to avoid worrying and overthinking.

• Make small targets for yourself. Your nervous mind can overthink things if you set goals that are too tall. Anxiety and overthinking find it difficult to set larger objectives. You will work your way up by setting lower targets.

•The value of meditation and mindfulness cannot be overstated. It helps with a variety of mental disorders, including anxiety and overthinking. As anxiety strikes, meditation will get you back to the current moment and help you relax.

•Determine the source of your nervous brain's overthinking. Triggers can exacerbate mental disorders, so investing time in writing down what causes fear and overthinking can help you control them.

•When it comes to paranoia and overthinking, distractions are crucial. Distractions can help reduce fear, depression, and other concerns, which is why you can finally start paying attention to your problems. Consider watching a movie or doing a jigsaw puzzle. Start noticing that you're getting the beginnings of a panic attack. Then try to get out of there as quickly as possible. Anxiety and overthinking can also be avoided, particularly if you are aware of the causes.

• If the fear and overthinking have been excessive and are consuming much of your best, it's time to get clinical help.

Anxiety and overthinking go hand in hand, so by controlling your anxiety and overthinking, you can significantly improve your situation.

Overthinking and Bipolar Disorder

When people think about bipolar disorder, they usually think about the mental health facts that they are familiar with. The health detail is the fact that people with bipolar disorder are either suicidal or psychotic. People who have it struggle with their attitude, but they can even struggle with overthinking.

Overthinking disturbing or distressing feelings is a common symptom of bipolar disorder on both sides of the coin. When someone is depressed, they will be concerned with what will happen in the future. They may also be concerned about the medication's side effects.

Mania will make it difficult to pay attention to your emotions, finding it difficult to question them. It's also difficult to tell the difference between reality and fiction. Alternatively, you can be so euphoric that you waste time in order to feel safe, only to regret it later.

It's important to get support from an anonymous or in-person doctor if you have bipolar disorder. For mild to severe conditions, online therapy is particularly effective. A psychiatrist can provide you with basic bipolar disorder statistics as well as mental health information. It's also important that you pay attention to your emotions.

Your bipolar spells will last for varying lengths of time, and your emotions can exacerbate them. You can obsess about the negative aspects of your condition, causing it to worsen over time. If we have bipolar disorder or not, the emotions that enter our heads seem to exacerbate the issue. If you need assistance, seek it.

Imaginative Positive Thinking

You may be perplexed as to how to avoid overthinking. One method is to think more positively. This will make you roll your eyes. You may believe that optimistic thoughts are, by definition, something you'd find in a cheesy health book.

Positive emotions and more positive thinking habits, on the other hand, are scientifically shown to be the keys to success. Here are few suggestions to help you think more positively.

• Examine your confirmation biases. Negative emotions are more likely to persist, while optimistic thoughts are more likely to go away. You should try to shift your perspective a little.

•Instead, begin to pay attention to the good feelings. Write down your good thoughts as soon as they occur to you. Take note of any good feelings you have and keep track of them.

•This cannot be emphasized enough. Make an effort to be conscious. You can learn to let go of some emotional pain using mindful strategies. The window is shattered by a malicious idea. Concentrate your views on the bright aspects.

•Consider how many times you've volunteered to assist others. Consider something that brings you joy. Allow some distressing thoughts to pass. It is a step-by-step procedure that requires repetition.

•Some people believe that constructive thinking entails no negative thoughts at all. Anything alarming should be overlooked, regardless of its magnitude. This is far from the case. In the overthinking department, thinking optimistic thoughts simply means doing less pessimistic thinking. Distressing feelings can arise, but constructive thinking shows us that personal pain is only fleeting and that there is much to be grateful for.

•Try cleaning up your social media feed. Remove the bad people from your life and concentrate on the positive. Yes, you can ingest bad news as well, however often people are overwhelmed by it, and it's not good for overthinkers.

Mentally Strong Individuals

Overthinking is less common in mentally strong individuals. Consider the brain to be a muscle. The more you train it, the stronger your mind can get. When you get older, it's becoming more necessary to strengthen your mental health. Mental health deteriorates as people age, but you can educate the mind with the right health facts.

Here are some helpful mental health tips for you:

• Mentally strong individuals engage in a variety of physical activities. When you think about fitness, you could picture powerful people working out to improve your body. Exercise, on the other hand, has a slew of mental health benefits. For eg, the brain releases feel-good chemicals that tend to suppress stress hormones while still killing pain. Not to mention, exercising will help you divert your attention away from your emotions, which is beneficial if you're trying to figure out how to avoid overthinking.

• People who are mentally strong try to socialize as much as possible. Try talking to a good friend to get to know them better. If you don't have any friends, go out and chat with someone in a bookstore, cafe, or any public place. When you're meeting new people and wanting to make friends, you're doing a lot less worried and a lot more about what's going on.

• Mentally strong people use cognitive behavioral therapy on a daily basis. This method of treatment aids in the elimination of negative behaviors and emotions and can be used to cure a variety of mental illnesses. Generalized anxiety disorder, bipolar disorder, eating disorders and other mental illnesses are among the most common.

• Strong people want to spice things up when it comes to emotional training. Repeating the same behavior will have certain harmful consequences. Consider a certain part of your life and consider what you should do better. Consider taking up a new passion, pursuing your dream career, or just discovering something new. It helps to stop overthinking as you start living for a new day.

• Strong people are certain that they can have moments of vulnerability. There are moments that you spend so much time concentrating, and you become aware that you are doing so. It'll happen, and there's no point in overthinking it. It occurs from time to time. Only don't devote a lot of time to it. You should set aside time to let your mind wander about a particular topic, and then avoid worrying about it when the timer goes off. This may require some practice, but powerful people will certainly give it a shot.

Stress Reduction

You may be wondering why "reduce tension" is on this list. Stress and our proclivity for overthinking go hand in hand. When we're in over our heads in a situation that scares us, our bodies respond with tension. But, our bodies can't say the difference between true danger and everyday issues, so the stress builds up.

People also find it difficult to deal with their pressures.

Any tension may be beneficial. Positive psychology-related stress, which is healthy stress, helps to challenge you and motivate you to do better. However, motivational psychology will only take you so far. Stress will exacerbate your troubles by making you fear disappointment, shame, loss, or losing everything you own.

• You obsess about the ones you can't alter. Most people understand that they can focus on the stuff they can control and disregard the things they can't, but it's difficult to avoid overthinking.

• Physical stress is a symptom of excessive stress. Every day is excruciating. Stress that causes physical discomfort is referred to as physical stress. Headaches and other body aches are examples of physical fatigue, which may also indicate clinical depression.

Anyone can experience stress. It makes no difference whether you're a kid, a teen, or an adult. Here are several basic stress-reduction techniques if you have a history of overthinking. Anyone can perform these basic methods, and they do not necessitate the assistance of a physician.

• Use cognitive-behavioral therapy (CBT). This is something that needs time to master, but learning to recognize unwanted feelings and how to deal with them is crucial.

• Make a list of the issues and rank them from most to least critical. Part of problem-solving entails starting with the most straightforward problem and working Problem-solving can become second nature to you in no time.

• Consider the feelings of loss and other common phobias. Why do you have such apprehensions about this? What effect does your depression have on you? If you have any fears, such as shame, loss, or anything else?

• People underestimate the importance of exercise. It will assist you in reducing depression by a small amount.

• Take a few moments to relax. Check out what's going on with your favorite show. Don't waste time procrastinating; instead, take a break and return with a new perspective.

• Avoid doing drugs or drinking beer. • Finally, consider consulting with a counselor if talking to a psychiatrist or psychologist leads to them prescribing medicine. They might be able to assist you with your issues.

Hypochondria is another aspect of overthinking and generalized anxiety disorder in general. This is because you always believe you have a medical condition, causing a major problem with overthinking.

Some may have a minor case of hypochondria. For example, you can believe something is wrong with you after consulting Dr. Google, so you consult your doctor. And you realize there's nothing wrong with you; it's just a case of overthinking combined with a touch of generalized anxiety disorder.

You might, however, be a hypochondriac to the extreme. You're still speaking with your doctor today to discuss something. You can have those thoughts after talking to the psychiatrist, and no amount of talking to your doctor seems to help them go away. You really believe you're sick, no matter how hard you try.

This is everything about which you can request assistance. There's a chance you're suffering from more than just generalized anxiety disorder. You will actually build up the nerve to admit that you're good by going to therapy.

Look for motivation.
Despite the fact that many people are wary of motivational speakers, they might be willing to assist you. Reading stories

about a man who overcame fear and lived, or people who learnt to survive at a later age, will inspire you and serve as a pleasant diversion from your overthinking.

It's a good way to learn more about mental health on a personal basis. Although any of this mental health knowledge might not be considered current psychology, it is worth investigating.

For health knowledge, Eckhart Tolle, a spiritual psychologist and author, is a good place to start. You inquire about Eckhart Tolle, a spiritual psychologist and author. Eckhart Tolle has published a number of books on living in the present moment, which is what most health advice about preventing overthinking focuses on.

Guy Winch, a counselor, is also worth listening to. Any author who specializes in emotional advice is worth reading.

When it comes to mindfulness, read everything you can on fitness. Some books are brief and can be read in a short amount of time. Others take a long time to complete, but the detail they have is well worth the wait. Self-help books can seem cheesy at first, but you'll be shocked at how much they can help with healing, disappointment, shame, loss, and other issues.

It's important to ingest as much mindfulness content as possible when it comes to overthinking. The trick to getting the assistance you need is mindfulness.

Is There Anything Else?

It's worth noting that much of how we think and how the brain functions are still unknown. Many research trials, both clinical and social, are available that could help us learn more about the mind. On the other hand, these clinical trials are exactly that: clinical, educational, and behavioral trials.

Maybe one day we will have a pill to cure overthinking that isn't subject to the same restrictions as clinical trials, but that day is quite a long way off.

Overthinking is a common occurrence that can happen at any moment. Overthinking may be a sign of anxiety or some form of anxiety disorder in people who suffer from it. Anxiety and stress over various circumstances and challenges in your life will easily devolve into overthinking and worrying about what you can do or how you could prevent bad things from occurring. You can't prevent any bad stuff from happening, and you can't prevent yourself from making a bad decision. What you should do is get assistance.

Here's How to Maintain A Positive Attitude

Life throws us crazy curveballs all the time, so here's how to remain calm no matter what.

1. Change your viewpoint

Changing your outlook on how you view life is the first step toward being positive. If you think anything is bad, it will most likely be (and vice versa). Embrace the mentality of a fixer and a doer to combat cynicism. There's always a way if there's a will! That is the true way to maintain a good attitude.

2. Take a Backward Step

Take a deep breath and a step back (or two). Let go of your negative energies, your frustration and disappointment, and concentrate on changing and finding the good. The light at the end of the tunnel is still there; you just have to look for it.

3. Be Conscious

Staying optimistic entails being self-conscious and aware of emotions. Allowing anxiety to take over and tell you that things will not turn out well is not a good idea. Accept the feedback that comes your way and remember that the majority of life's events aren't personal.

4. Foster a positive atmosphere

Make a healthy atmosphere for yourself. Surround yourself with people who will help you develop, who will love you, and who just want the best for you. Avoid putting yourself in positions that don't contribute to your satisfaction and they're a waste of time.

5. Take It Slowly

Take it easy on yourself and don't be too harsh on yourself. It takes time to develop the ability to remain optimistic. Trust that if you wait long enough, your persistence and optimism will pay off, and that good thing will come your way when the time is right.

6. Encourage Others to Be Positive

It all continues by taking positivity to everyone when it comes to being optimistic. Be compassionate with others, polite, and open-minded, and all of that positive energy will undoubtedly return to you.

7. having a healthy body leads to having a healthy mind.

The mind-body relation is undeniable, and it's crucial when it comes to satisfaction. Working out on a daily basis, maintaining a nutritious diet, meditating, and having enough sleep (at least 7 hours) are all excellent ways to promote a healthier body and mind.

8. Make Gratitude a Habit

Gratitude for what we have will make us see how many wonderful things we have in our lives and reflect on the positive. We'll never get anywhere if we focus on our troubles and what we don't have. Keep a grateful journal or blog to express your gratitude on a regular basis, even for the smallest of items.

9. Appreciate the beauty of nature

Nature is a wonderful way to remain happy and add more joy to your life. If you're feeling sad, spending some time outside in the fresh air is still a smart idea. It has been discovered that we respond best in natural settings, and that spending time in nature can relieve tension while still increasing imagination. According to a study conducted in Finland, city dwellers that walked through nature for even twenty minutes a day were less depressed than those who walked through the city.

10. Exclude Materialism and Ideals

Our modern culture instills in us the belief that in order to be a respectable human, we must be a certain way and own certain expensive, material possessions. But, before social media and entertainment, we didn't need those justifications. Get rid of your beliefs and concentrate on what you are, rather than what you believe you should be.

11. Put on some music

Music is an excellent way to add more positivity to your life! There are a plethora of feel-good tracks and playlists available that will get you humming and partying in no time, forget about whatever it was you were mad about in the first place. Listening to music activates dopamine, the feel-good hormone in the brain, which is a biological reality.

12. Make a happy face!

You smile when you're pleased. But, believe it or not, smiling makes you happier as well. And if you don't feel like it, practice smiling. Look in the mirror and tell yourself that you have a perfect, broad grin. When it comes to being optimistic in a stressful world, smiling is important.

13. Follow Your Dreams

Do what you want to do! You must surround yourself with stuff and people that make you feel happy if you want to be optimistic. If creative writing is your passion, for example, go for it! Make time for the things that bring you pleasure, even though they aren't your current work.

14. Participate in a Support Group

It's difficult to be alone. Having a support network with which you can express your thoughts can be very helpful in discovering new strategies for being motivated no matter what.

What Are the Advantages of Maintaining a Positive Attitude?

There's no denying that being optimistic will help you in all aspects of your life.

It has been discovered that being happy improves one's health and lengthens one's life. In reality, it's been discovered that people with a good outlook will extend their lives by up to ten years!

For those who have feelings like gratitude and admiration, being optimistic has been seen to assist with career development, team bonding, financial achievement, and even athletic results.

When it comes to friendships, happy people seem to have more, which is important for success and longevity. Couples that have a higher positive-to-negative relationship ratio seem to live longer.

How to Maintain a Positive Attitude at Work

With endless pressures surrounding you and perhaps coworkers who don't necessarily see eye to eye with you, it can be difficult to remain optimistic at work.

It's important to change the way you think about your career in order to remain positive at work:

• No matter what comes your way, spread love, affection, and positive vibes in the workplace.

• If anything irritates you, take a moment to pause before responding. Our immediate responses aren't really the most positive.

• To stop getting overloaded, listen to others, be open-minded, and stay on top of the duties.

How to Maintain a Positive Attitude during The Job Search

Although getting a career can be very difficult, not having one at all can be much more so. It's difficult to keep your chin up through a work hunt that seems to have no end in sight.

Here's how to keep your spirits up through your career search:

• Don't cover up your emotions, and don't be afraid to express them to your friends and family; they'll be able to help you get through this tough period.

• Be honest in your expectations and don't expect anything to happen immediately. Finding a decent career takes time, but if you wait long enough, something good will come along.

• As you begin your work quest, try to establish a schedule for yourself so that you feel efficient and inspired to get out of bed every morning.

Rules for Putting the Best Effort into It

After someone attempts to do something and fails, one of the first things I always learn is that they tried their hardest. It's comforting to remember that, even though you didn't get what you wanted, you gave it you're all to achieve. But what does it entail to provide it with you're all?

My interpretation of doing your utmost seems to vary from that of many others. I've seen a lot of people try half-heartedly to do something just to brag about how hard they worked. However, to me, giving it your all means doing whatever you can to make things possible.

Making an Effort

There will be several times where I put in a strong effort to excel in anything only to fall short. Maybe my skills aren't up to par, or maybe my timing is wrong. There may be a variety of reasons why I wasn't able to pull it off. My only fear is that one of the causes isn't that I didn't do my hardest.

I despise the idea of failing at anything just because I didn't do anything possible to make it happen. There could have been moments when I could have succeeded if I had given it my all. It seems that failing to give it my all is a means of squandering chances.

But I've made a list of rules that I follow to ensure that I'm still giving it my all.

1. Put everything you've got into it.

The first rule of giving it your all is to make sure you're giving it your all. While it seems to be a straightforward concept, most people overlook it. Trying the hardest means that you put in your best effort. Anything less than that indicates that you aren't doing anything you can.

Anything less than 100% might be the reason you don't excel. If you're just offering 90 percent or even 95 percent to yourself, the extra 5-10 percent might be the difference between success and failure.

2. Experiment many times

It seems futile to give up after the first try. It means that any of the subsequent efforts will still fail, which isn't always the case.

It's like a guy who asks a girl out once and is turned down. As a result, he comes to the conclusion that it won't work out with any other women, anywhere. That doesn't make much sense at all.

Trying the hardest necessitates multiple attempts rather than just one. In most fields, rejection is an inevitable part of the equation. When this happens, that doesn't mean you won't try again.

3. Have in mind to self-reflect.

This law is closely related to the second. You don't want to keep doing the same tasks over and over again while you're making several efforts to do something. Self-reflection is needed to get the most out of each attempt.

Self-reflection will reveal possible opportunities for change, allowing you to devise new ideas and approaches to explore next time.

You should get as much feedback as possible after each unsuccessful attempt. What went wrong? What went wrong, and when did it go wrong? All of this experience will be used to boost the next try, improving your chances of success.

4. Seek advice.

Getting input from others is not only a smart thing, but it is frequently needed. If you know someone who has already seen success with everything you wish to do, their wisdom will be invaluable.

They will give you new perspectives and point out things that you would otherwise overlook. Maybe they've noticed something about you or your strategy that might be better. Many times, until anyone points it out to you, you might not even notice it.

5. Want to be hopeful about the chances of success.

Pessimism is dangerous. Once you've thought about all the negative stuff that will almost certainly happen, you'll start looking for opportunities to make them happen.

You ensure that all those negative feelings don't sabotage your attempts by remaining positive. When you're doing the hardest, the last thing you need is your own pessimistic feelings getting in the way.

6. If you fail, do so in a respectful way.

And if you put in your best effort, you will always fall short. Because of this tragic fact, any loss can be emotionally damaging.

The crucial thing to note is to accept your loss with dignity. Allowing mistakes to overwhelm you is a bad idea. It's possible that you didn't excel due to a cause outside your influence. It is possible that you will never remember.

Of necessity, the need to be angry will exist. Consider all of the American Idol contestants who scream furiously after being told their singing is bad. Don't be that way.

7. Still exude self-assurance.
Whatever you do, strive to exude as much confidence as possible. That goes with cases where you're completely terrified of failing.

If you present yourself as someone who lacks trust, you won't get too far. If you have to, fake faith. Faking trust will ultimately aid in the development of genuine confidence.

Everyone has doubts, but you can't let them get in the way of your success. When you allow doubt to creep in, you'll begin to make more mistakes, and failure will become inescapable.

How to Get Rid of Your Perfectionism

Are you a perfectionist? How to Stop Being Your Own Worst Enemy in 10 Easy Steps

Here are ten things perfectionists can do to keep themselves motivated and get more out of life:

1. Make your personal goals and expectations more realistic.

Recognize that you are already sufficient and that you do not need to be perfect to achieve your objectives.

Setting more realistic goals will free up energy that would otherwise be spent attempting the impossible, resulting in a more balanced lifestyle.

2. Refute negative thoughts by challenging your inner critic.

Allowing your motivation to be the cause of your demise is not a good idea. Instead of allowing your inner voice to wreak havoc on your emotional well-being, it's critical to use healthy rewards and positive feedback to achieve your goals.

Reduce the volume of negativity in your life, amplify your intuition, and let positivity and love lead you to success and fulfillment.

3. Make self-care a priority and make an investment in yourself.

Before attempting to assist the person next to you, put on your own gas mask. Participate in therapy, rekindle an old hobby, and keep reading so that you can better care for yourself and others.

4. Make it a habit to say no more frequently.

Due to their high ambition, perfectionists often struggle to say no to new opportunities; however, healthy boundaries are the very thing that leads to long-term energy.

Stop assuming extra tasks that aren't directly related to your passion so that you can focus on what really matters.

5. it's important to remember that time off isn't time wasted.

When you're in the mindset of an overachieving perfectionist, it's easy to dismiss relaxation as a waste of time. It's important to remember, however, that sleeping and doing light-hearted activities are both healthy and necessary ways to re-energize your motivation.

Practice relaxing and recharging your batteries so that you can keep pursuing your goals.

6. Have faith that everything will be completed on time.

You know how to complete any task because you've been doing it your whole life. You know you'll finish a project and it'll be spotless by the time you're done, even if it means staying up all night and putting yourself through hell.

Use that knowledge to feel more at ease when you're feeling overwhelmed—no there's a need to panic when your track record suggests you'll succeed.

7. Take a break and recharge your batteries.

Rather than thinking, "I'll take some time off when it feels right," go the extra mile and make relaxation a priority. You're probably a Type A personality who needs to put self-care first or else it won't happen.

Consider how different your life would be if you put half as much effort into relaxation as you do in other areas.

8. Take a weekend trip to get away from it all.

There's nothing quite like getting out of town and immersing yourself in new surroundings. When you travel to new places, you cleanse your energy and release the emotional and mental baggage that comes from working too hard in the same place for too long.

9. Stop wasting time by doing multiple things at once.

You think you're an outlier when it comes to multitasking, but you're not. Stop attempting to do too many things at once; it not only wastes energy, reduces efficiency, and impairs memory, but it also adds to the stress you already have.

Begin meditating and allow that state of mind to accompany you throughout the day.

10- Experiment with not holding others to the same standard like yourself.

It's easy to fall into the trap of expecting others to perform at the same level as you when everything you do is flawless. The rest of the world isn't wired the same way you are, which is unfortunate or fortunate depending on your point of view.

What Is Failure Fear?

If you're afraid of failing, you'll avoid potentially dangerous situations.

Fear of failure prevents you from trying, instills self-doubt, stymies progress, and may lead you to compromise your values.

What causes apprehension about failure? The following are the main reasons why people are afraid of failing:

Childhood Recurrences

Children internalize harmful mindsets as a result of hypercritical adults' ultimatums and fear-based rules. As a result, children feel compelled to ask for permission and reassurance all of the time. This need for approval follows them into adulthood.

Perfectionism is the pursuit of perfection.

Fear of failure is often at the root of perfectionism. Perfectionists fear failure so much that they don't even try. Getting out of your comfort zone can be frightening.

Over-Personalization is a term that refers to the process of personalizing

We may over-identify with failures as a result of our ego. It's difficult to see past failure and consider things like effort quality, extenuating circumstances, or growth opportunities.

False Self-Assuredness

True confidence recognizes that they will not always succeed. A person with shaky self-esteem avoids taking risks. They'd rather play it safe than the risk it all.

How Fear of Failure Keeps You from Achieving Your Goals

Unhealthy Workplace Culture

A culture of perfection exists in far too many organizations today: a set of organizational beliefs that any failure is unacceptable. Only unadulterated success will suffice.

Imagine the anxiety and fear in such an organization. Constant concealment of even the tiniest flaws. The wild finger-pointing as everyone tries to blame someone else for the inevitable messes. Lying, cheating, falsifying data, and burying problems until they become crises that can no longer be hidden.

Don't Let Valuable Opportunities Pass You By

Many more people fail because of their ego-driven commitment to what worked in the past, if some people fail to reach a complete answer because of the lure of some early success. This is common among senior executives, particularly those who rose to prominence by pioneering significant change years ago.

They are hesitant to try new things because they are afraid that if they do, it will tarnish the luster they have built up around their names as a result of previous triumphs.

Furthermore, the reason, the success of something new may even demonstrate that their previous accomplishments were not so great after all. Why take a chance when you can keep your reputation intact by doing nothing?

Such people are so invested in their egos and past glory that they would rather pass up opportunities for future glory than risk even the possibility of failure.

Losers Became High Achievers

Every talent has an antonym, which can be problematic at times. People who are effective enjoy winning and setting big goals. This can leave them so afraid of failing that their lives are ruined. When a good attribute, such as success, becomes overly prominent in a person's life, it is on the verge of becoming a huge roadblock.

Many successful individuals place a high emphasis on achievement. It's what they've built their lives around. They excel in all areas of their lives: education, college, athletics, the arts, hobbies, and jobs. Each new accomplishment heightens the significance of the importance of their lives.

Failure gradually becomes unimaginable. Perhaps they've never struggled before with something they've attempted, because they've never had to overcome adversity. Failure becomes their worst fear, something they must escape at all costs.

The only way to do this is never to take a chance, to adhere rigidly to everything you know you should do, to defend yourself, to work the longest hours possible, to double and triple check all, and to be the most diligent and conservative individual on the planet.

If relentless diligent work, persistence, brutal work hours, and harrying subordinates aren't enough to hold the risk of failure at bay, try something else. Falsify numbers, mask bad information, disguise mistakes, ignore consumer reviews, and constantly pass the responsibility for errors onto someone who is too poor to fight back.

Suffering from a Lack of Creativity

Overachievers jeopardize their own mental health as well as the lives of others who work for them. People who are too concerned with "righteousness" and justice become self-righteous bigots. Those whose ideals for developing intimate relationships become unbalanced seem to suffocate their friends and relatives with endless displays of affection and requests for love in exchange.

All want to be successful. The issue arises when fear of disappointment becomes overwhelming. You are unable to consider the inevitability of making errors and the importance of trial and error in seeking the most innovative alternative.

The most inventive you are, the more mistakes you can make. Making the decision to stop making mistakes would also destroy your imagination.

Balance is more important than you would imagine. The sweetest dish has a little tang to even it out. A little selfishness is valuable even in the most caring person. And a little setback is necessary to keep everyone's outlook on progress intact.

We learn a lot about how important it is to be optimistic. Perhaps we will need to acknowledge that the negative aspects of our lives and experiences are equally important in achieving achievement in work and in life.

How to Get Rid of the Fear of Failure (Step-by-Step)

1. Determine the source of the fear.
Consider what might be the source of the pessimistic belief.

Which of the four major reasons for a fear of failure can you relate to the most?
Write down where you believe the anxiety stems from and learn to comprehend it from the outside.

Imagine you're attempting to assist one of your closest friends if it works. Perhaps you're afraid because of something that happened to you as a kid, or because you're insecure.

When you name the root of your anxiety, it loses some of its strength.

Reframe Your Goal-Oriented Beliefs

Having an all-or-nothing mindset will also leave you with nothing. Get a good idea of what you want to do, but don't forget to include discovering something new in your plan.

You are much less likely to fail if you constantly strive for progress and learning.

In order to remain on the cutting side, they promote experimentation and invention. Failure is a part of the mentality, but as long as they fulfill their goal of telling amazing tales, all of the setbacks are just opportunities to improve.

Develop a Positive Mental Attitude

You believe what you say yourself in certain ways. How you respond and respond is influenced by your internal conversation.

Our culture is fixated on achievement, but it's important to remember that even the most prosperous people struggle.

A newspaper once fired Walt Disney because they said he lacked talent. He moved on to open a bankrupt cartoon factory. Disney is now a household name since he never gives up.

Steve Jobs was once sacked from Apple before returning as the company's face for a long time.

Disney and Jobs would not have succeeded if they had believed the poor reviews.

It's up to you to pay attention to your derogatory self-talk and recognize stimuli.

Make a visual representation of all possible outcomes.

It's scary to be unsure of what will happen next. Take the time to consider the various consequences of your choice. Consider the best-case and worst-case scenarios. If you've always had a chance to brace for what could happen physically, you'll feel better.

Fear of the unknown may prevent you from accepting a new position. Consider the advantages and disadvantages, as well as future gains and defeats, when making such a life-changing decision. Knowing how things could turn out might assist you in getting unstuck.

Consider the Worst-Case Situation

There are moments when the worst-case scenario could be disastrous. When something negative happens, it isn't really the end of the planet.

In the grand scheme of things, it's important to define how horrific the worst-case situation is. We grant circumstances more strength than they warrant at times. In the vast majority of situations, the loss is not irreversible.

Starting a new company, for example, is bound to be a learning process. You'll make choices that don't work out, but the pain is usually just temporary. You have the option to change your plan and recover. Even if the perceived loss resulted in the closure of the company, it might serve as a springboard for something better.

Conclusion

Overthinking occurs when you think too hard instead of behaving and doing stuff. Overthinking occurs as you consider, comment about, and repeat the same ideas hyper and over instead of behaving. You are unable to take responsibility because of this habit. It drains your vitality, impairs your ability to make choices, and traps you in a never-ending cycle of thought and thinking. This is a way of thought that drains your time and resources while still preventing you from acting, doing new things, and progressing throughout your life. It's like tying yourself to a pole with a cord and going in circles over and over again.

There are some methods for breaking this practice, including watching television, playing video games, or listening to music. Walking, cycling, or other forms of physical activity will momentarily divert your attention away from your habit of overthinking. Something that keeps your mind busy with something that prevents you from overthinking is appropriate. When you overthink, keep track of how much time and resources you're wasting and how passively you're acting instead of aggressively. Recognize that thought once, or even a few times, is sufficient. It gets you nowhere if you keep thinking the same thoughts over and over. You must make a decision and take action.

CPSIA information can be obtained
at www.ICGtesting.com
Printed in the USA
BVHW080020190521
607637BV00004B/582

9 781802 710649